40 DAYS

OF

RESURRECTION APPEARANCES

THE CHRONOLOGY OF JESUS' LIFE – PART 3

JOHN MAXWELL

Special thanks

All glory and honour to God and special thanks to my beautiful wife Yeng, my father and mother, John and Eileen, Charles Harbottle, Austin McDermott, David Goodship and Raja Natarajan for all their love, help, support, and prayers.

40 DAYS OF RESURRECTION APPEARANCES

ISBN 9798372723160

Published 2023

Edited by Austin McDermott

Contents

Introduction

The most important events in the history of the world are the death, burial and resurrection of Jesus Christ, the Son of God. All events in history prior to them, led to that point and all events since then have led from that point.

The Gospels say he died on Friday at Passover; was buried before the Sabbath began at sunset and rose on the third day according to the Scriptures. Then he made these appearances over forty days:

Matthew 28:1-20

Jesus appeared to women from Galilee at the empty tomb
Jesus gave the Great Commission on a Galilean mountain

Mark 16:1-20

Jesus appeared to Mary Magdalene at the empty tomb
Jesus appeared to two disciples in the countryside
Jesus appeared to his disciples as they were eating
Jesus gave the Great Commission and ascended to heaven.

Luke 24:1-53 and Acts 1:1-11

Jesus appeared to two disciples on the road to Emmaus
Jesus appeared to Peter
Jesus appeared to his disciples in the house in Jerusalem
Jesus told his disciples to stay in Jerusalem
Jesus ascended into heaven from the Mount of Olives

John 20:1-21:23

Jesus appeared to Mary Magdalene at the empty tomb
Jesus appeared to his disciples in the house in Jerusalem
Jesus appeared to his disciples and Thomas in the house
Jesus appeared to seven disciples by the Sea of Galilee

Also, 1 Corinthians 15:5-7 records five resurrection appearances:

1 Corinthians 15:5-7

Jesus appeared to Peter
Jesus appeared to the Twelve
Jesus appeared to more than five hundred believers
Jesus appeared to James
Jesus appeared to all of the Apostles

The order of resurrection appearances

The Gospels and 1 Corinthians 15:5-7 record twenty appearances that Jesus made to his disciples over the forty-day period after he rose from the dead. First it will be shown which writers recorded the same appearances then the order that the appearance happened will be established. Then each appearance will be examined to find when it occurred so it can be set correctly in the forty-day timeframe of his appearances. The timing of Jesus' appearances and the time between them will enable us to see more clearly the impact they had on his disciples and what that means to us today.

To set resurrection appearances into forty, day-by-day segments, the best approach is to believe what is written in the Bible. It was the method used to write, 'The Jesus Diary'[1], Part One of the Chronology of Jesus' Life series. It resulted in the fullest chronology of events of his life ever written. Events for each of the forty days are recorded with an explanation as to how its chronology was established. A more detailed explanation is given in the Appendix.

Jesus rose on the third day (Luke 24:21) after dying at the Passover, which fell on a Friday (John 18:28 and John 19:31). Passovers were held on only two Fridays in this period of history: – 7/4/30 and 5/4/33. In 'The Jesus Diary,'[1] it was shown God's Son died for the sins of the world on Friday, 7/4/30 and rose three days later, on Sunday, 9/4/30. After forty days of resurrection appearances, he ascended to heaven on Thursday, 18/5/30. So the crucified and risen Son of God appeared to his disciples from 9/4/30 to 18/5/30.

6

Historical evidence of Jesus

Before we begin this day-by-day journey let's look at records outside the Bible that show Jesus was a real figure that existed in history. The Gospels say Jesus was killed by Pontius Pilate, the governor of Judea in the reign of Roman Emperor Tiberius. Historical evidence for events in his reign is scarce. Only four historians wrote about his reign and two of them mention Jesus. Tacitus mentions him directly and Suetonius mentions him indirectly. This is not the Bible or some Christian writer, but historical texts of the events of Tiberius' reign.

It is surprising any Roman historian should mention Jesus. He was a Jewish preacher who was crucified in Israel, a far flung part of their Empire. Tacitus and Suetonius did not write about him because they were interested in him. They wrote about Jesus because of the quantity of Christians in the Empire. There were tens of thousands of them and they were a problem to the leaders. When they examined where they all came from and why they were disturbing the Empire, Roman historians traced it all back to one man, Jesus of Nazareth, who was crucified by Pontius Pilate. Christians came from Jesus.

Suetonius

Roman historian, Suetonius wrote about Jesus because the number of Christians in the Empire was a problem. In his history of Rome's Emperors, 'The Lives of the Caesars'[2], he wrote the following:

'The Jews were constantly making disturbances at the instigation of Christus (his term for Christ). And because of this man Christ there was so much trouble Claudius expelled all the Jews from Rome.'[2]

It is a well-established historical fact that in 43AD, Emperor Claudius drove all of the Jews out of Rome, because they were having big fights and quarrels over this man called Jesus Christ. The writings of Roman historian, Suetonius confirm this historical fact. He was not the only Roman historian to write about Jesus of Nazareth.

Tacitus

The Roman historian Tacitus wrote about events in Nero's reign. In May 64AD Rome caught fire destroying ten of its provinces and Nero was the main suspect. He wanted to knock down the city and rebuild it to his own design. When people blamed him for the fire, he blamed the Christians to get himself out of trouble. He said there were so many of them and they predicted that one day the world would end by fire – a day of judgment by fire. When Nero said the Christians started the fire to bring about the end of the world, Tacitus wrote:

'Nero fastened the guilt on a class hated for their abominations called Christians by the populace. Christus from whom the name originated, suffered the extreme penalty in Tiberius' reign at the hands of Pilate, a most mischievous superstition, thus checked for the moment broke out not only in Judea, the source of the evil but even in Rome.'[3]

This is not the Bible or early Christian writing, it is Roman historian, Tacitus' writing. His unsympathetic reference to Jesus and the Christians says their name came from the historical person, Christus or Christ in Latin, who suffered the extreme penalty (crucifixion). He says Pilate authorised it in the reign of Tiberius. It affirms what the Gospels say about Jesus' death. After Nero accused the Christians, he tortured masses of them (not for arson, but for being enemies of the human race). In their death they were made the subject of sport, killed by animals in arenas. They were nailed to crosses and set on fire. So many Christians were burned; it lit Rome's streets at night.

The historical accounts say Christians filled the Roman Empire. When their historians investigated where all the Christians came from they would have read the records that Pilate had sent back from Israel to Rome. In those records they would have traced the source of where all the Christians came from to Jesus of Nazareth whom Pilate had crucified in the reign of Emperor Tiberius. However, it was not only Roman historians who wrote about him, Jewish ones did as well.

Josephus

Jewish historian Josephus wrote of Jesus. The text may have been corrupted in later translations but it does not diminish proof of Josephus' writing confirming Jesus' existence. He wrote:

'Now there was about this time, Jesus, a wise man, if it be lawful to call him a man, for he was a doer of wonderful works – a teacher of such men as receive the truth with pleasure. He drew over to him both many of the Jews and many of the Gentiles. He was Christ; and when Pilate, at the suggestion of the principal men amongst us had condemned him to the cross, those that loved him at first did not forsake him, for he appeared to them alive again the third day, as the divine prophets had foretold these and ten thousand other wonderful things concerning him; and the tribe of Christians so named after him, are not extinct to date.' [4]

The Jewish Rabbis

Even the Jewish rabbis wrote about Jesus. The Rabbinical writing found in the ancient Babylonian Talmud says:

'Jesus the Nazarene, they hanged him on Passover Eve'. [5]

These Jewish rabbinical leaders knew the date and the time Jesus died. The Jewish leaders did not want him crucified on Passover day. But, because Pilate slowed things down, Jesus died at the exact time the Passover lambs were slaughtered.

So there is proof of Jesus' existence in historical records outside of the Bible. However, it is the Gospel and New Testament accounts that we will rely on to establish both Jesus' resurrection and the timeframe of events during his forty days of appearances. If the New Testament is to be used as the source for establishing the timing of his appearances, it is vital to establish the reliability of its content.

The reliability of the Gospels

Jesus' existence is confirmed by the writings of Roman and Jewish historians, but can what the Gospels say about him be trusted? As they were written so long ago, some may say the material is not reliable. We know what the Gospel writers wrote is unchanged over time through the science of 'Textural Criticism'. Essentially, this science says, the more texts that are in existence and the closer to the events they were written, the less doubt there is about the authenticity of the original text. Writer FF Bruce shows how rich the New Testament is in manuscript attestation by comparing the texts with other classic historical works in his book, *'Are the New Testament Documents Reliable?'*[6]

Bruce shows there are only about ten copies of Caesar's Gallic War in existence and the oldest text was written nine hundred years after Caesar died. There are just twenty copies of Livy's Roman History in existence today. The earliest text was written over nine hundred years after events occurred. Of the fourteen books of the Histories of Tacitus, only twenty copies survive today. Ten portions of the sixteen books of Tacitus' Annals depend entirely on two manuscripts. One of which was written in the ninth Century and the other manuscript was written two hundred years later, in the eleventh Century.

There are eight manuscripts of the History of Thucydides, written around 900AD, which was more than thirteen hundred years after those events occurred. There are around eight copies of the texts of the History of Herodotus and they were written over thirteen hundred years after the events took place. However, no classical scholar doubts the authenticity of these historical works despite the low number of manuscripts and the very large gaps between the events taking place and the time when the manuscripts were written. However, unlike these ancient classics there is a wealth of New Testament documents written soon after the events took place.

A wealth of New Testament manuscripts

The New Testament was written from 40AD-100AD. However, there are manuscripts dating from 350AD (a time span of only 300 years from the time of the original events). Papyri containing most of the New Testament writings date from the third century and there is a fragment of John's Gospel dating from 130AD. There are over 5,000 Greek manuscripts, over 10,000 Latin manuscripts, 9,300 other manuscripts and over 36,000 other citings in the writings of the early Church fathers. One of the best textural critics of all time, FJA Hort commented on this wealth of texts:

'In the variety and fullness of evidence on which it rests, the text of the New Testament stands absolutely and unapproachably alone among ancient prose writing.'[7]

FF Bruce summarises the evidence by quoting Sir Frederick Kenyon, a leading scholar in this area:

'The interval then between the dates and the original composition and the earliest external evidence becomes so small as to be in fact negligible, and the last foundation for any doubt that the Scriptures have come down to us substantially as they were written have now been removed. Both the authenticity and the general integrity of the books of the New Testament may be regarded as finally established.'[8]

With such an abundance of texts written so soon after the events and with the endorsement of leading scholars in the field, it is clear that the texts of the New Testament are accurate and reliable. These confirmations give the confidence to use the information recorded in the Gospels to establish the timing of the events of Jesus' forty days of resurrection appearances.

Resurrection Day

Sunday, 9/4/30

Women visited the tomb

Matthew 28:1 says after the Sabbath, at dawn on the first day of the week, Mary Magdalene and the other Mary visited the tomb. The Sabbath is Saturday; the last day of the Jewish week and Sunday is the first. If Jesus died on Friday, 7/4/30, he rose on Sunday, 9/4/30 and the women went to the tomb at dawn that day. The Jerusalem solar calendar says that dawn breaks at 05:50 Hours[a] on the Ninth of April in the current year. The time that dawn breaks has not changed over the years. If dawn breaks at that time today, it would have broken at 05:50 Hours on the day that Jesus rose from the dead.

An angel rolled the stone from the tomb

As the women from Galilee went to the tomb, there was an earthquake as an angel from heaven came and rolled back the stone from the entrance to Jesus' tomb then sat on it. The angel's appearance was like lightning, and his clothes were as white as snow. The guards at the tomb were so afraid they became like stone. The angel said to the women, *"Do not be afraid, for I know you are looking for Jesus who was crucified. He is not here; he has risen, just as he said. Come, see the place where he lay. Then go quickly and tell his disciples, 'He has risen and is going ahead of you into Galilee. There you will see him.' Now I have told you."* (Matthew 28:2-7).

Resurrection Day – Sunday, 9/4/30

The Jewish leaders had persuaded Pilate to seal and guard Jesus' tomb (Matthew 27:62-66), so nobody could have entered it to steal the body before the angel rolled the stone away. Jesus definitely died on the cross, because Pilate checked with the centurion in charge of his crucifixion that he was dead, before he released Jesus' body to Joseph to bury it (Mark 15:42-45). So he could not have resuscitated himself and come out of the tomb. He was dead and buried. By all accounts his body should have been there, but when the stone was rolled away it was not. Jesus had risen to life. The stone was not rolled away to let him out (his resurrected body could pass through walls), it was rolled away to let witnesses to his resurrection in.

Peter received a special mention

Mark 16:7 says the angel told the women to tell the disciples and Peter that Jesus was going ahead of them to Galilee and they would see him there. Even though Peter had deserted Jesus and denied him three times, he was still on God's heart and that morning he received a special mention. Isn't God great? It doesn't matter how much we mess up in life, and Peter had messed up, God never stops loving us and we are always on His mind and on His heart.

Risen Jesus appeared to the women

The women, afraid, yet filled with joy, heeded the angel's words and ran back to the city to tell his disciples Jesus had risen. Whilst they were on their way risen Jesus suddenly appeared and greeted them. They came to him, fell on their knees, clasped his feet and worshipped him. Then Jesus said to them, "*Don't be afraid. Go and tell my brothers to go to Galilee; there they will see me.*" So according to Matthew 28:8-10, the women were the first ones to see risen Jesus. On the night before he died he called his disciples, 'friends not servants' (John 15:15). However, in his risen form, he called his disciples, 'brothers'. Jesus' death and resurrection elevated the status of their relationship to the highest level.

Resurrection Day – Sunday, 9/4/30

The priests bribed the tomb guards

After the women left, the tomb guards went into the city and told the priests everything that had happened. The chief priests met with the elders and devised a plan. They gave the soldiers a large sum of money and told them to say Jesus' disciples had come during the night and stolen him away. They reassured the soldiers that if the report got to Pilate, they would satisfy him and keep them out of trouble. The soldiers took the money and did as they were instructed (Matthew 28:11-15). It is interesting that the leaders who had seen Jesus die, used the word, 'him' and not, 'his body' when devising their account of his missing body. And if the guards were asleep how could they see his disciples or anyone steal his dead body? These events would have happened soon after dawn on Resurrection Day.

Peter and John visited the empty tomb

When the women returned from the tomb, they told the Eleven and all the others who were in the house in Jerusalem all they had seen and heard, but they did not believe them, because their words seemed like nonsense. Peter and John ran to the tomb and inside they saw the strips of linen Joseph and Nicodemus had wrapped around Jesus' dead body (John 19:38-42) lying there as though he had passed right through them. The burial cloth from around Jesus' head lay nearby, folded up neatly by itself, separate from the linen. John saw and believed, but he and Peter still did not understand from the Scriptures that Jesus had to rise from the dead (Luke 24:9-12 and John 20:2-9).

Everything recorded at the tomb that day reveals details of Jesus' resurrected body. He rose and left the tomb before the angel rolled the stone away. Death could not hold his body. His resurrected body could pass through material things, such as the linen strips and the rock wall of his tomb. The neatly folded cloth around his head shows his new body was not ghostlike and could handle material things.

Resurrection Day – Sunday, 9/4/30

Risen Jesus appeared to Mary Magdalene

After Peter and John had returned to the house, Mary stood outside the tomb crying. '*As she wept, she bent over to look into the tomb, and saw two angels in white, seated where Jesus' body had been, one at the head and the other at the foot. They asked her, "Woman, why are you crying?" "They have taken my Lord away," she said, "and I don't know where they have put him." At this she turned around and saw Jesus standing there, but she did not realise it was Jesus. "Woman," he said, "Who are you looking for?" Thinking he was the gardener, she said, "Sir, if you have carried him away, tell me where you have put him and I will get him." Jesus said to her, "Mary." She turned and cried out in Aramaic, "Rabboni!" (which means Teacher). Jesus said to her, "Do not hold on to me, for I have not yet returned to the Father. Go instead to my brothers and tell them, 'I am returning to my Father and your Father, to my God and your God.'" Mary went and told the disciples, "I have seen the Lord!" And told them all he had said*' (John 20:10-18).

In her search for Jesus, Mary does not mention his name once. She was so in love with him and enamoured by him, she assumed the angels and 'the gardener' knew who she meant. Mary's theology may not have been correct (she had not taken to heart Jesus' words about him dying and rising again), but her heart was right – it was full of love for her Lord. And Jesus responded to Mary's love for him. It seems he interrupted his return to his Father to appear to her. It is a wonderful demonstration of Jesus' love for his disciples. It did not matter if her theology was incorrect. It did not matter that she had not remembered or taken to heart the words he had spoken to her. Jesus responded to the love for him that filled her heart to overflowing. Like Mary Magdalene, we can take comfort in the fact that our theology does not have to be perfect to be in this loving relationship with Jesus Christ, the Son of God, who is God.

Resurrection Day – Sunday, 9/4/30

The angels sat where Jesus' body had been, one at the head and the other at the foot – like the cherubim on the cover of the Ark of the Covenant watching over the Mercy Seat in the temple in Jerusalem (Exodus 25:17-22). The blood the chief priest sprinkled there each year on the Day of Atonement atoned for his sins and the sins of the Jewish people. In the tomb, the angels were seated where the slain Lamb of God had lay. Jesus' blood and death, once and for all atoned for every sin, ever committed by everyone, past present and future. The fact the angels were seated implies the atoning work for sin was finished, once and for all. Nothing more could be added to it.

Risen Jesus appeared to Peter

1 Corinthians 15:5 says after Jesus died and rose on the third day according to the Scriptures, he appeared to Peter. On Resurrection Day, he appeared to two disciples at Emmaus (see below). The pair hurried back to Jerusalem to tell the Apostles they had seen Jesus and added he had appeared to Peter (Luke 24:34). If they saw Jesus in the afternoon of Resurrection Day and immediately returned to the capital to tell the apostles, Jesus could not have been seen by Peter during the road to Emmaus appearance. Jesus must have appeared to Peter before he met the two disciples on the way to Emmaus.

Peter did not see Jesus at the tomb when he ran to it with John. And he had not seen Jesus prior to that; otherwise he would not have run to the tomb to check what the women had said was true. He must have appeared to Peter after he was seen by Mary Magdalene, and before he met the disciples on the road to Emmaus. The Holy Spirit has chosen to keep the contents of this meeting between the risen Lord and Peter secret. John 21:1-23 records the time when he saw Jesus by the Sea of Galilee and he was restored to his ministry. So we can assume that at this personal appearance on Resurrection Day, Peter, who had deserted Jesus and denied him three times, was restored personally from his emotional pain and shame.

Resurrection Day – Sunday, 9/4/30

Risen Jesus appeared at Emmaus

Now that same day, two disciples were going to a village called Emmaus, about seven miles from Jerusalem. As they discussed with each other everything that had happened, Jesus himself came up and walked along with them, but they were kept from recognising him. He asked, "What are you discussing together as you walk along?" They stood still, their faces downcast. Cleopas, asked him, "Are you only a visitor to Jerusalem and do not know the things that have happened there in these days?"

"What things?" he asked. "About Jesus of Nazareth," they replied. "He was powerful in word and deed before God and the people. Our religious leaders handed him over to be sentenced to death and they crucified him, but we had hoped he was the one who would redeem Israel. What is more, it is the third day since all this took place. In addition, some women amazed us. They went to the tomb at dawn but did not find his body. They told us they had seen a vision of angels, who said he was alive. Then some companions went to the tomb and found it just as they had said, but him they did not see." He said to them, "How foolish you are, and how slow of heart to believe all the prophets have spoken. Did not the Christ have to suffer these things then enter his glory?" And beginning with Moses and all the Prophets, he explained all the Scriptures concerning himself.

As they reached Emmaus, Jesus acted as if he was going further. But they urged him to stay with them as it was nearly evening, the day was over. So he went with them. At the table he took bread, gave thanks, broke it and gave it to them. Then their eyes were opened and they recognised him, and he disappeared from their sight. They asked, "Were not our hearts burning within us while he talked with us on the road and opened the Scriptures to us?" They left and returned at once to Jerusalem' (Luke 24:13-33).

Resurrection Day – Sunday, 9/4/30

The importance of seeing Jesus in the Scriptures

The disciples told Jesus about events that had occurred in Jerusalem (Luke 24:18-24). Though they were heading in the wrong direction – away from the action, he, in his great love came to them. He walked with them and listened to their concerns, but they were kept from recognising him as he explained all the Scriptures concerning himself. In Jesus' eyes, it was more important for them to see and recognise him in the Scriptures than it was for them to see and recognise him in person. And today we are no less disadvantaged than they were on the road to Emmaus. The same Scriptures (the Bible) are available to us today and the same Jesus is there to be seen and recognised in the written word. It was only as he broke bread at the house in Emmaus that the pair's eyes were opened and they saw it was him. All Scriptures point to Jesus and his death and resurrection. Breaking bread at Communion celebrates his selfless sacrifice that ransomed us, healed us, restored us and forgave all our sins.

The template for a church service

The appearance at Emmaus is the perfect template for a church service. It takes place on the first day of the week, Sunday. There is testimony from the members. In the main talk, Jesus is revealed in the Scriptures. When that happens, the listeners' hearts are set on fire. Afterwards, bread is broken as Jesus' loving sacrifice on the cross is remembered. As he was revealed to the disciples at Emmaus when he broke bread, remembering his crucifixion reveals the true heart and character of God's Son Jesus and God Himself. What is more, the revelation of Jesus will, like the disciples that day prompt us to tell others. They hurried back to Jerusalem – to the place he wanted them to be. And Jesus will deal with us in the same way today if we head in the wrong direction. He will come alongside us and listen to our concerns. He will reveal himself to us through the Scriptures and in Communion then when we see Jesus, we will be back on track.

Resurrection Day – Sunday, 9/4/30

Risen Jesus appeared to the Apostles

'They (the two disciples) *got up and returned to Jerusalem. There they found the Eleven and those with them, assembled together in the Upper Room in the house. They told them, "It is true! The Lord has risen and has appeared to Simon." Then the pair told them what had happened on the way to Emmaus and how Jesus was recognised by them when he broke the bread.*

While they were still talking about this, Jesus himself stood among them even though the doors were locked in fear of the Jews. Jesus said to them, "Peace be with you!"

They were startled and frightened, thinking they had seen a ghost. He said to them, "Why are you troubled and why do doubts arise in your minds? Look at my hands and my feet. It is I myself! Touch me and see; a ghost does not have flesh and bones, as you see I have."

When he had said this, he showed them his hands and feet. And while they still did not believe it because of joy and amazement, he asked them, "Do you have anything here to eat?" They gave him a piece of broiled fish, and he took it and ate it in their presence.

He said to them, "This is what I told you while I was still with you: Everything must be fulfilled that is written about me in the Law of Moses, the Prophets and the Psalms.

Then he opened their minds so they could understand the Scriptures. He said, "This is what is written: The Christ will suffer and rise from the dead on the third day, and repentance for the forgiveness of sins will be preached in his name in all nations, beginning in Jerusalem. You are witnesses to these things."' (Luke 24:33-48).

Resurrection Day – Sunday, 9/4/30

Jesus is the centre

When Jesus appeared to his disciples in the house, he came and stood in the middle of them. Throughout his ministry he stood in the midst of the crowds (Mark 3:9). Even in his death Jesus was crucified in the middle of two criminals (Mark 15:27). When the disciple John saw Jesus in heaven, he saw a lamb who had been slain at the centre of the throne. In heaven, Jesus is enthroned in the centre, surrounded by all the heavenly beings (Resurrection 5:6-12).

Jesus loves to be at the centre of everything and he loves to be at the centre of everything in our lives. The Lord longs to be the centre of our marriages, our families, our homes, our friendships, our jobs, our finances and every other aspect of our lives. He loves us, but he will never force his way into our lives. He longs to be at the centre of everything. The world was created by him. It functions best when it is Christo-centric. We were made by him and we function at our best when we are Christo-centric. Life functions at its fullest when we have Jesus at the centre of our lives. He longs to be at the centre of them, but we have to invite him in. If we put him at the centre of our lives, we will live in the fullness of life that Jesus Christ came to bring when he brought the kingdom of God to this Earth.

The importance of Holy Communion

Jesus was revealed to the two disciples at Emmaus when he broke bread. He appeared to his apostles in the Upper Room as the two described how they had seen him when he broke bread. There is no insignificance in the fact that Jesus was seen when bread was broken in remembrance of him. God loves us to recall the death and resurrection of His Son – because the heart of God – the heart of our heavenly Father, His Son Jesus and the Holy Spirit – and the fullness of the character of the Triune God are revealed in the death of Jesus Christ, the Son of God on the cross at Calvary.

Resurrection Day – Sunday, 9/4/30

Jesus' peace is the antidote to fear

The disciples had stayed in the house in Jerusalem out of fear of the Jews since Jesus died (John 20:19). When he appeared to them, he said, "*Peace be with you*" - twice (John 20:19 and John 20:21). His peace is the best antidote for fear. It was for the disciples that night and it is for us today. Because Jesus died for our sins, we have peace with God. He has given us His peace. If we rest in His peace, nothing in this world will frighten us. God freely gives us His peace in Jesus. All we have to do is receive it and remain in it.

Jesus' wounds are the divine receipts

The next thing Jesus did was to show his disciples the nail holes in his hands and feet and the hole from the spear in his side. They had seen him nailed to the cross. They had seen him die on the cross. They had seen the soldier pierce his side with a spear. You might say, "Only John was at the Crucifixion." However, Luke 23:49 says, *'But all those who knew him, including the women who had followed him from Galilee, stood at a distance, watching these things.'* Scripture cannot lie. *'All those who knew him'* included his disciples. In 1 Peter 5:1, Peter himself declared he was a witness of Christ's sufferings. Jesus was showing them and us his wounds. They are the divine receipts that the debt for our sins has been paid in full. If Jesus Christ died for the sins of the world on Friday, 7/4/30 then the Son of God would have risen from the dead on Sunday, 9/4/30.

Thought

If you struggle to believe in Jesus' Resurrection so did his disciples

Day 2

Monday, 10/4/30

Jesus' disciples stayed in Jerusalem

John 20:26 says it was one week after Jesus' first appearance to his disciples in the house in Jerusalem when he appeared to them again there, but where were they during that week? On Resurrection Day, an angel and Jesus told the women to tell his disciples to go to Galilee, where they would see him (Matthew 28:5-10). John 21:1-23 records they saw Jesus by the Sea of Galilee and he re-instated Peter in his ministry. Matthew 28:16-20 records he appeared to them on a mountain in Galilee and gave them the Great Commission to make disciples of all nations. However, did their journey to and from Galilee and the appearances there take place in the week between Jesus' two appearances to his disciples in the house in Jerusalem?

In my book, 'The Jesus Diary'[1] it was shown fit men like the disciples could walk twenty-five miles in a day. The pace would drop over longer distances to about twenty miles a day. Galilee was over ninety miles from Jerusalem. The walk to Galilee would have taken them five days if they walked at twenty miles a day, and it would have taken five days to return to Jerusalem. There was not enough time (7 days) between the two appearances to his disciples in the house in Jerusalem for them to make a round trip to Galilee.

Day 2 – Monday, 10/4/30

Let us see if the Gospels reveal where the disciples were between Jesus' first two appearances. John 20:26 says a week after his first appearance they were in the house again with the doors locked. When Jesus appeared to them the first time in the house, the doors were locked in fear of the Jews (John 20:19). According to John's record it seems their situation had not changed over the week. They were still in Jerusalem. They were still in the house behind locked doors. By all accounts it would seem they were still living in fear of the Jews. From this it can be assumed they spent the week locked in the house for fear of the Jews. If that is correct, it would mean the disciples spent Monday, 10/4/30 locked in the house in Jerusalem.

Day Two of the Feast of Unleavened Bread

Jesus was crucified on Friday, 7/4/30. That day, the Passover and the Sabbath began at sunset (John 18:28 and John 19:31) and ended at sunset on Saturday, 8/4/30. The Feast of Unleavened Bread began at sunset that day. It remembered Israel's forty years of Exodus in the desert. A holy assembly was held on the first and last days of the feast when no regular work was allowed (Leviticus 23:5-8). Day One of the feast lasted from sunset on Saturday 8/4/30 until sunset on Sunday 9/4/30, the day Jesus rose to life. Day Two of the feast would have been celebrated on Monday, 10/4/30.

Thought

Fear of man will prove to be a snare but whoever trusts in the Lord is kept safe

Day 3

Tuesday, 11/4/30

Jesus' disciples stayed in Jerusalem

After Jesus appeared to his disciples five times on Resurrection Day; the Gospels record the following appearances: John 20:26-29 says Jesus appeared to them again in the house in Jerusalem one week after his first appearance to them. Then John 21:1-23 says he was seen by them by the Sea of Galilee. Matthew 28:16-20 says Jesus appeared to them on a mountain in Galilee. Luke 24:49 says he told them to stay in Jerusalem to receive the Spirit. Then Luke 24:50-53 and Mark 16:19-20 say the disciples witnessed his ascension from the Mount of Olives on his fortieth day of appearances (18/5/30). So the disciples must have gone to Galilee after Thomas saw Jesus and before he told them to stay in Jerusalem to receive the Holy Spirit.

Capernaum was about ninety miles from Jerusalem. If the disciples walked at about twenty miles a day, it would have taken five days to reach Galilee and another five to return to the capital. The round trip would have taken ten days; besides the time they spent in Galilee. If Jesus first appeared to them in the house on Sunday, 9/4/30; and his next appearance there was a week later, on Sunday, 16/4/30, there was not enough time between these two appearances (7 days) to make a ten-day round trip from Jerusalem to Galilee.

Day 3 – Tuesday, 11/4/30

At Jesus' first appearance to his disciples in the house in Jerusalem, the doors were locked out of fear of the Jews (John 20:19). At Jesus' second appearance to them in the house one week later, they were still in the house and again the doors were locked (John 20:26). It seems that the disciples' situation had not changed over those seven days. They were still locked in the house, apparently still living in fear of the Jews. If that is correct, then Jesus' disciples would have spent Tuesday, 11/4/30 locked in that house in Jerusalem.

Day Three of the Feast of Unleavened Bread

Jesus died for our sins on Friday, 7/4/30. The Passover and Sabbath began at sunset that day (John 18:28 and John 19:31) and ended at sunset on Saturday, 8/4/30. Then the Feast of Unleavened Bread began. The seven day feast remembered Israel's forty years of Exodus in the desert. A holy assembly was held on the first and last days of the feast. No regular work was allowed on those two days (Leviticus 23:5-8). Day Three of the feast would have been held from sunset on Monday, 10/4/30 to sunset on Tuesday, 11/4/30, whilst the disciples remained locked in the Upper Room in Jerusalem.

Thought

Do not be afraid of those who can kill the body but cannot kill the soul

Day 4

Wednesday, 12/4/30

Jesus' disciples stayed in Jerusalem

The day Jesus rose from the dead (Sunday, 9/4/30), he appeared to his disciples five times. First, he appeared to women from Galilee at the empty tomb (Matthew 28:8-10). He appeared to Mary Magdalene next (John 20:10-18). Then Jesus appeared to Peter (Luke 24:34) and to two disciples at Emmaus (Luke 24:13-32). Next he appeared to the apostles in the house in Jerusalem (John 20:19-23). Thomas was not there that night. It was a week later at his sixth appearance after Jesus rose from the dead that Thomas along with the others saw their Lord in the house in Jerusalem (John 20:24-29).

It seems the disciples spent the seven days in between Jesus' first two appearances to them, in Jerusalem. This was despite Jesus' and the angel's instructions to them on Resurrection Day (given to the women from Galilee at the empty tomb) to go to Galilee where they would see him. Resurrection Day was also the first day of the Feast of Unleavened Bread. The feast lasted seven days. It was one of three feasts that God commanded all Jews to attend each year in Jerusalem (Deuteronomy 16:16). In obedience to God's command, the disciples would not have left Jerusalem until after the Feast of Unleavened Bread had ended at sunset on Saturday, 15/4/30.

Day 4 – Wednesday, 12/4/30

Sunday, 16/4/30 was the earliest Jesus' disciples could have left the capital to go to Galilee. They did not leave that day. John 20:26-29 says Jesus appeared to them in the house in Jerusalem that night. John 20:26 adds that the doors were locked. When Jesus appeared to them the first time in the house in Jerusalem, John 20:19 says the doors were locked for fear of the Jews. According to John, it seems their situation remained unchanged over the seven days. Jesus' disciples were still in Jerusalem. They were still in the house behind locked doors. By all accounts it would seem they were still living in fear of the Jews. From this it can be assumed they spent the week in Jerusalem, locked in the house for fear of the Jews. It would mean they spent Wednesday, 12/4/30 locked in the house in the capital.

Day Four of the Feast of Unleavened Bread

Jesus was God's Passover lamb. The Passover and the Sabbath began at sunset on Friday, 7/4/30 (John 18:28 and John 19:31), the day he died on the cross of Calvary for the sins of the world. When the Passover feast ended at sunset on Saturday, 8/4/30, the Feast of Unleavened Bread began. The feast remembered Israel's forty years of Exodus in the desert. A holy assembly was held on the first and last days of the seven-day feast. No regular work was allowed on those two days (Leviticus 23:5-8). Day Four of the feast would have been celebrated in Jerusalem from sunset on Tuesday, 11/4/30 to sunset on Wednesday, 12/4/30, whilst the disciples stayed in the house.

Thought

Do not be afraid little flock for the Father is pleased to give you the kingdom

Day 5

Thursday, 13/4/30

Jesus' disciples stayed in Jerusalem

Jesus rose from the dead on Sunday, 9/4/30 and he appeared to his disciples over a period of forty days before ascending into heaven. On Resurrection Day, he appeared to his disciples five times in and around Jerusalem. His sixth appearance to his disciples was also in the capital. John 20:26 says Jesus appeared to them in the house in Jerusalem one week after his first appearance, which would have been Sunday, 16/4/30. Thomas was absent at his first appearance, but he was present in the house one week later.

After Jesus died for our sins on the cross, Joseph of Arimathea and Nicodemus placed his dead body in the tomb before the Sabbath began at sunset. That Friday (7/4/30), the Passover feast also began at that time (John 18:28 and John 19:31). When those holy days ended at sunset on Saturday, 8/4/30, the Feast of Unleavened Bread began. It lasted seven days. It was one of the feasts God commanded all Jews to attend each year in Jerusalem (Deuteronomy 16:16). In obedience to God's word, Jesus' disciples would have remained in the capital. They would not have been able to leave for Galilee until the feast ended on Saturday, 15/4/30. The earliest they could have left Jerusalem was Sunday, 16/4/30.

Day 5 – Thursday, 13/4/30

Matthew 28:5-10 says on Resurrection Day, Jesus and an angel at the empty tomb told the women from Galilee to tell his disciples to go to Galilee where they would see him. Also, on the night before he died, he told his disciples he would go ahead of them to Galilee after he had risen from the dead (Mark 14:28). Despite all these instructions, they stayed in Jerusalem until he appeared again in the house a week after his first appearance (John 20:26-29).

When he appeared to them the second time, the doors of the house were locked, just as they had been at his first appearance. John 20:19 says the doors were locked the first time for fear of the Jews. It was the fear that the Jewish religious leaders and those in Jerusalem might do to the disciples what they had done to Jesus. From John's record, it seems that they spent the week locked in the house living in fear of the Jews. It would mean the disciples spent Thursday, 13/4/30 locked in the Upper Room in the house in Jerusalem.

Day Five of the Feast of Unleavened Bread

Jesus was God's Passover lamb. The Friday that he died, the Feast of Passover and the Sabbath began at sunset that very day, 7/4/30 (John 18:28 and John 19:31). It ended at sunset on Saturday, 8/4/30 then the Feast of Unleavened Bread began. The seven-day feast remembered Israel's forty years of Exodus in the desert. A holy assembly was held on the first and last days of the feast. No regular work was allowed on those days (Leviticus 23:5-8). Day Five of the feast would have been held from sunset on Wednesday, 12/4/30 to sunset on Thursday, 13/4/30 as the disciples remained in the house.

Thought

The Lord is my helper I will not be afraid. What can man do to me?

Day 6

Friday, 14/4/30

Jesus' disciples stayed in Jerusalem

After Jesus, the Son of God died for the sins of the world and was buried on Friday, 7/4/30; he rose from the dead on the third day, Sunday, 9/4/30. On Resurrection Day, Jesus appeared five times to his disciples. His final appearance that day was to ten apostles and the other disciples gathered in the house in Jerusalem. Thomas was absent (John 20;24) and Judas Iscariot was dead (Matthew 27:5).

Jesus' next appearance, which was his sixth to his disciples was also in that house in Jerusalem a week later (John 20:26). Even though Jesus had told them to go to Galilee after he had risen from the dead (Matthew 28:8-10) they could not have gone there and returned to the capital between those two appearances as there was not enough time. Also, the Feast of Unleavened Bread began on the day Jesus rose from the dead. As it was one of the three feasts God told all Jews to attend each year in Jerusalem (Deuteronomy 16:16), the disciples would have remained in the capital until the seven-day feast ended on Saturday, 15/4/30. The earliest they could have set out to Galilee would have been on Sunday, 16/4/30. However, as Jesus appeared to them that day, they must have stayed in Jerusalem between those first two appearances to the disciples in the house.

Day 6 – Friday, 14/4/30

At Jesus' second appearance to his disciples on Sunday, 16/4/30, John 20:26 says they were in the house with the doors locked. When he appeared to them the first time, John 20:19 says the doors were locked in fear of the Jews. According to John's record it seems their situation had not changed over the week. They were still afraid the Jewish leaders and those attending the feast would do to them what they had done to Jesus, if they found out they were his disciples. So, a week after Jesus' first appearances, the disciples were still behind locked doors in the house in Jerusalem. Friday, 14/4/30 would have been one of the days when they remained locked in the house.

Day Six of the Feast of Unleavened Bread

Jesus was God's Passover lamb. On the day God's Son was crucified, Friday, 7/4/30, the Feast of Passover and the Sabbath began at sunset (John 18:28 and John 19:31). When the two holy days ended at sunset on Saturday, 8/4/30, the Feast of Unleavened Bread began. The seven-day feast remembered Israel's forty years of Exodus in the desert after God had freed them from slavery in Egypt. A holy assembly was held on the first and last days of the feast when no regular work was allowed (Leviticus 23:5-8). Day Six of the feast would have been held from sunset on Thursday, 13/4/30 to sunset on Friday, 14/4/30, whilst his disciples remained in Jerusalem.

Thought

Do not fear for I am with you

Day 7

Saturday, 15/4/30

Jesus' disciples stayed in Jerusalem

The first Sabbath that was celebrated after Jesus rose from the dead on Sunday, 9/4/30 was held on Saturday, 15/4/30. It was a holy day of rest when no regular work was permitted (Exodus 20:8-11). That day was the final day of the seven-day Feast of Unleavened Bread. It too was a holy day of rest when no work was permitted. This feast was one of three that God commanded all Jews to attend each year in Jerusalem (Deuteronomy 16:16). In obedience to God's word and as walking long distances was considered as work, Jesus' disciples would have been unable to set out from Jerusalem on their five-day walk to Capernaum in Galilee that Saturday.

Jesus' disciples would have remained where they were that day. It seems from John's Gospel, that was the Upper Room in the house in Jerusalem. When Jesus first appeared to them in that house on Resurrection Day, John 20:19 says they were in the house behind locked doors out of fear of the Jews. When Jesus appeared to them there again one week later, John 20:26 says they were still locked in the house. So, it seems that for the first eight days of Jesus' forty days of resurrection appearances, the disciples stayed locked in the house in Jerusalem out of fear of the Jews.

Day 7 – Saturday, 15/4/30

Day Seven of the Feast of Unleavened Bread

The first day of the seven-day Feast of Unleavened Bread was Resurrection Day, Sunday, 9/4/30. The final day of the feast which commemorated Israel's forty years of Exodus in the desert was a holy assembly (Leviticus 23:5-8). Day Seven of the feast would have been held from sunset on Friday, 14/4/30 to sunset on Saturday, 15/4/30, as the disciples stayed locked in the house.

Sabbath celebration in Jerusalem

Jesus rose from the dead and appeared to his disciples on the first day of the Hebrew week (Luke 24:2), which was Sunday, 9/4/30. Six days later would have been the final day of the Hebrew week: Saturday, 15/4/30. It was a Sabbath when no work, which included walking long distances was permitted (Leviticus 23:3). The holy day would have been celebrated from sunset on Friday, 14/4/30 to sunset on Saturday, 15/4/30. Jesus' disciples would have remained in the house in Jerusalem on the Sabbath.

<u>Thought</u>

Fear stops us stepping out

Day 8

Sunday, 16/4/30

Risen Jesus appeared to Thomas

'Thomas, one of the Twelve, was not with the disciples when Jesus came, so the other disciples told him, "We have seen the Lord!" But Thomas said to them, "Unless I see the nail marks in his hands and put my fingers where they nails were, and put my hand into his side, I will not believe it." A week later they were in the house again and Thomas was with them. Though the doors were locked, Jesus came and stood among them saying, "Peace be with you!" Then Jesus said to Thomas, "Put your finger here; see my hands. Reach out your hand and put it into my side. Stop doubting and believe!" Thomas declared to him; "My Lord and my God!" Then Jesus told Thomas, "Because you have seen me, you have believed, blessed are those who have not seen me and yet have believed."' (John 20:24-29).

Mark 16:14 and Luke 24:33-36 both say Jesus first appearance was to the Eleven, yet Thomas was absent (John 20:24) and Judas had killed himself (Matthew 27:3-5). It means only ten of the original twelve apostles were present at that first appearance. Either the apostles were called the Eleven, whether they were all there or not, or the writers included Matthias, who replaced Judas as the twelfth apostle after Jesus ascended to heaven (Acts 1:15-26).

Day 8 – Sunday, 16/4/30

Thomas must have been so disappointed when he learned Jesus had appeared to the others whilst he was out of the house. Because he declared he would not believe unless he put his fingers in the nail marks in his hands and put his hand in the hole in his side, he became known as, 'Doubting Thomas'. His torment of not seeing Jesus alive after he had risen from the dead lasted seven more days.

If Jesus appeared to his disciples in Jerusalem on Sunday, 9/4/30, then he would have been seen by them and Thomas, one week later in the house, on Sunday, 16/4/30. He told Thomas to put his finger in the hole in his hand and to put his hand in the hole in his side. He told him to stop doubting and believe. It made Thomas declare Jesus was his Lord and his God. His angst of having to wait a week longer to see Jesus was replaced by his joy of acknowledging he was God. His waiting on God's timing achieved a greater purpose than seeing Jesus had risen. It revealed he was the Son of God who is God.

Thomas should be remembered for this and not for his doubting. It is crucial to wait on God's timing and not miss His bigger purpose. Jesus did this when he raised Lazarus from the dead. If he had not waited two days after hearing Lazarus was ill (John 11:6), it would have been another healing. Waiting on God's timing not only raised Lazarus to life, but it revealed Jesus as the Resurrection and the Life. At this second appearance in the house in Jerusalem, the dynamic of Jesus' deity entered his disciples' belief system through Thomas' revelation.

Thought

Our strength will rise as we wait upon the Lord and it will reveal a bigger purpose in our lives

Day 9

Monday, 17/4/30

The disciples' journey to Galilee

On Resurrection Day (Sunday, 9/4/30), the angel at the empty tomb and Jesus told the women from Galilee to tell his disciples to go to Galilee where they would see him (Matthew 28:5-10). However, the disciples stayed in the house in Jerusalem until Jesus had appeared to Thomas a week after he first appeared to them in Upper Room in the city on Sunday 16/4/30 (John 20:26-29). After that appearance; John 21:1-23 says Jesus appeared to Peter and six other disciples by the Sea of Galilee and he restored Peter to his ministry as head of his Church. Matthew 28:16-20 says risen Jesus appeared to the apostles on a mountain in Galilee where he gave them the Great Commission to make disciples of all nations.

The earliest the disciples could have travelled to Galilee was the day after Jesus had appeared to Thomas, which was, Monday, 17/4/30. Acts 1:3-12 says the final time they saw him was at his ascension from the Mount of Olives on his fortieth day of appearances, on Thursday, 18/5/30. If the disciples returned to Jerusalem by Wednesday, 17/5/30 at the latest having set out on the five-day walk from Galilee on 13/5/30, their visit to Galilee and Jesus' appearances there would have taken place from 17/4/30 to 12/5/30.

Day 9 – Monday, 17/4/30

Jerusalem was ninety-odd miles from Galilee. If they walked at twenty miles a day, it took five days to walk there and five to return. Walking long distances was unlawful on Sabbaths (Leviticus 23:3), so they could not have travelled on the Sabbaths celebrated on 22/4/30; 29/4/30; 6/5/30 and 13/5/30. If they rested on those days, it leaves three periods when they could have made unbroken five-day walks from Jerusalem to Galilee then back to the capital:

Possible timeframes of their journeys

Monday, 17/04/30 to Friday, 21/04/30
Sunday, 30/04/30 to Friday, 05/05/30
Sunday, 07/05/30 to Friday, 12/05/30

They could not have walked to Galilee from 7/5/30 to 12/5/30, as it did not leave enough time for appearances there and a return journey to Jerusalem to occur before the Ascension on 18/5/30. If they went to Galilee from 30/4/30 to 5/5/30, it left one day (6/5/30) for events there to occur before they returned to Jerusalem in the last unbroken period, 7/5/30 to 12/5/30. Jesus' appearance by the lake lasted two days. It began on the night of one day and ended in the morning of the next day (John 21:1-4), so they could not have gone to Galilee from 30/4/30 to 5/5/30. The only time Jesus' disciples could have made an unbroken journey to Galilee was from 17/4/30 to 21/4/30.

Jericho was the last town Jesus visited before arriving in Jerusalem for Holy Week (Luke 19:1-28). If his disciples followed this route home, it would have been their first stop on the way. If they left Jerusalem the day after Thomas saw Jesus, they would have spent Monday, 17/4/30 walking to Jericho and spent the night there.

Thought

A Christian does not hide in the crowd

Day 10

Tuesday, 18/4/30

Journey from Jericho to south Samaria

Galilee was ninety-odd miles from Jerusalem. If fit young men like the disciples could walk twenty miles in a day, it would have taken five days to reach Galilee. As the Feast of Passover was one of the feasts Jews had to attend in Jerusalem each year (Deuteronomy 16:16), they would have been unable to return to Galilee until the feast ended on 15/4/30, as it was unlawful to walk long distances on holy days. The earliest they could have left the capital was the day after Thomas saw Jesus. The latest they could have returned there was the day before the Ascension (17/5/30). Due to the Sabbaths held on 22/4/30; 29/4/30; 6/5/30; and 13/5/30 in the period:17/4/30-17/5/30, plus the duration of events in Galilee, the only time Jesus' disciples could have made an unbroken journey from Jerusalem to Galilee (without resting on a Sabbath) was from 17/4/30 to 21/4/30.

Jericho was the last town Jesus and his disciples visited before they arrived in Jerusalem for Holy Week (Luke 19:1-28). If they took this route to Galilee, Jericho would have been the first town they visited on the way home. If they left Jerusalem early on Monday, 17/4/30, the fifteen-mile walk would have seen them arrive in Jericho before sunset and they would have spent the night in that city.

Day 10 – Tuesday, 18/4/30

During his ministry, Jesus went through Samaria as he returned from Jerusalem to Galilee. When he returned from the Judean countryside before his Galilean ministry began, he visited Sychar in Samaria (John 4:3-42). In his final year of ministry, Jesus went through Samaria on the way to Jerusalem and spent the night in a Samaritan village near the Galilee border (Luke 9:51-56). It was over forty miles to walk from Jericho, through Samaria, to that border.

If Jesus walked at about twenty miles a day, the journey would have taken him at least two days to complete. He would have spent the first day walking about twenty miles through south Samaria. Before sunset, he would have stopped in a town or village in that region and spent the night there. Next morning, he would have set out and spent the day walking from the village or town where he stayed in south Samaria to the border of Galilee. He would have arrived there before sunset and spent the night in a town or village in the border area.

If the disciples took the same route from Jerusalem to Galilee, then their journey through Samaria would have taken two days. They would have set out first thing in the morning after spending the night in Jericho. They would have spent all of Tuesday, 18/4/30 walking around twenty miles through the region of southern Samaria. Then they would have stopped at a town or village in that region before the sun set and would have stayed the night there.

Thought

Following in Jesus' footsteps is always the best route to take

Day 11

Wednesday, 19/4/30

Journey from south Samaria to north Samaria

Galilee was about ninety miles from Jerusalem. If fit young men like the disciples could walk twenty miles in a day, it would have taken five days to reach Galilee. As the Feast of Passover was one of the feasts Jews had to attend in Jerusalem each year (Deuteronomy 16:16), they would have been unable to return to Galilee until the feast ended on 15/4/30. Jesus appeared to Thomas on 16/4/30, so the earliest they could have left the capital for Galilee was the next day. The latest they could have returned to Jerusalem was the day before the Ascension (17/5/30). Due to the Sabbaths in that period and the duration of events in Galilee, the only time they could have made an unbroken walk to Galilee was from 17/4/30 to 21/4/30.

Jericho was the last town Jesus and his disciples visited before he arrived in Jerusalem for Holy Week (Luke 19:1-28). If they followed the same route home, it would have been the first town they visited on the way to Galilee. The fifteen-mile walk would have taken the disciples most of the day. If they set out from Jerusalem in the morning of Monday, 17/4/30, they would have arrived in Jericho the same day and they would have spent the night there.

Day 11 – Wednesday, 19/4/30

After the Passover following Jesus' baptism and temptation; he stayed in the Judean countryside. When he returned to Galilee, he travelled through Samaria and stopped at a town called Sychar (John 4:3-42). Luke 9:51-56 says he passed through Samaria on his final journey to Jerusalem and the cross of Calvary. Jesus and his disciples spent the night in a village in the border region of Galilee and Samaria. It was over forty miles from Jericho to the border of Samaria and Galilee. A journey of that length would have taken Jesus at least two days to complete. If the disciples took the same route to Galilee, their journey would have taken two days as well.

They would have set out first thing in the morning after spending the night in Jericho. The disciples would have spent Tuesday, 18/4/30 walking about twenty miles through the region of southern Samaria. Then they would have stopped at a town or village in that area before sunset and stayed the night there. They would have left the town or village that they stayed in, first thing the next morning. They would have spent all of Wednesday, 19/4/30 walking about twenty miles to the region of northern Samaria. The disciples would have stopped at a town or village close to the border of Samaria and Galilee before sunset and they would have spent the night there.

Thought

Everyone who drinks this water will be thirsty again, but whoever drinks the water I give him will never thirst

Day 12

Thursday, 20/4/30

Journey from north Samaria to Nazareth

Galilee was about ninety miles from Jerusalem. If Jesus' disciples walked at about twenty miles in a day, it would have taken them five days to arrive in Capernaum. They would have left Jerusalem on Monday, 17/4/30, the day after Jesus appeared to Thomas. Because of the Sabbaths that were celebrated in the period after he appeared to Thomas and before his ascension into heaven (17/4/30-17/5/30) and the duration of events in Galilee, the only time they could have made an unbroken journey to Galilee was from 17/4/30 to 21/4/30.

Jericho was the last town that Jesus and his disciples visited before they arrived in Jerusalem and the events of Holy Week began. If the disciples followed the same route to Galilee, Jericho would have been their first stop on the way home (Luke 19:1-28). The fifteen-mile walk to Jericho would have taken the disciples most of the day. If they set out from Jerusalem in the morning of Monday, 17/4/30, they would have arrived in Jericho before sunset that same day and they would have spent the night there. They could have stayed at Zacchaeus' home in Jericho. Jesus brought salvation to this tax collector as he made his final journey to Jerusalem (Luke 19:1-10).

Day 12 – Thursday, 20/4/30

During his time of ministry, Jesus travelled from Jerusalem through Samaria to Galilee, stopping in villages on the way (John 4:3-42). On his final journey to the capital, he passed through Samaria and spent the night in the border area (Luke 9:51-56). It was over forty miles from Jericho, through Samaria, to the border of Galilee. The journey would have taken Jesus at least two days. If the disciples took the same route, their journey would have taken at least two days.

If they left Jericho early on Tuesday, 18/4/30 they would have spent that day walking about twenty miles through south Samaria. Before sunset, they would have stopped in a town or village in that area and spent the night there. They would have set out next morning and spent all of Wednesday, 19/4/30 walking about twenty miles through Samaria to the Galilee border. The disciples would have stopped at a town or village in that area before sunset and spent the night there

On Thursday, 20/4/30 they would have crossed the Galilean border and spent the day walking through south Galilee. Before sunset, the disciples would have stopped in a town or village there and spent the night there. If they followed Jesus' route, they would have stayed in Nazareth. He went there in his final two years of ministry (Mark 6:1-6 and John 7:1-10) on his way to the Feast of Tabernacles. At Jesus' crucifixion, he placed Mary into John's care (John 19:25-27). John would not have left Mary and her family in Jerusalem, at the mercy of the leaders who had Jesus killed. He and the other disciples would have taken Jesus' family with them to Galilee. If that is so, it is likely Mary would have invited them to stay at her home in Nazareth.

Thought

Unless you people see miraculous signs and wonders you will never believe

Day 13

Friday, 21/4/30

Journey from Nazareth to Capernaum

Galilee was about ninety miles from Jerusalem. The disciples could walk up to twenty-five miles in a day, but that pace would drop to about twenty for longer distances. If they walked at that pace, it would have taken five days to reach Galilee. If Thomas saw Jesus on Sunday, 16/4/30, the earliest they could have left Jerusalem was Monday, 17/4/30. To witness the Ascension, they would have returned to the capital by Wednesday, 17/5/30 at the latest. Due to the Sabbaths held in the timeframe, 17/4/30 to 17/5/30 and the duration of events in Galilee, the only time they could have made an unbroken journey from Jerusalem to Galilee was from 17/4/30 to 21/4/30.

The last town that Jesus visited before arriving in Jerusalem for Holy Week was Jericho (Luke 19:1-28). If Jesus' disciples followed the same route home, it would have been the first town they visited. The fifteen-mile walk would have taken most of the day. If they set out from Jerusalem early on Monday, 17/4/30, then they would have arrived in Jericho before sunset that day and they would have spent the night there. The disciples may have stayed at the home of Zacchaeus, to whom Jesus brought salvation as he made his final journey to Jerusalem and the cross of Calvary (Luke 19:1-10).

Day 13 – Friday, 21/4/30

During his ministry, Jesus walked through and stayed in Samaria as he returned to Galilee from Jerusalem (John 4:3-4). Luke 9:51-56 says he passed through and stayed in Samaria on his final journey to Jerusalem. It was over forty miles from Jericho to Galilee's border. If the walk took him two days, it would have taken the disciples two days if they took that route. If they left Jericho early on Tuesday, 18/4/30, they would have spent that day walking about twenty miles through south Samaria. Before sunset, they would have stopped in a village in that area and spent the night there. Next day, the disciples would have set out and spent Wednesday, 19/4/30 walking about twenty through Samaria to the Galilee border. They would have stopped in a village in the border area and spent the night there.

Next day, they would have set out early. After crossing the border they would have spent all of Thursday, 20/4/30 walking through south Galilee. They would have stopped and spent the night in a village there. If they followed Jesus' route they would have stayed in Nazareth. He went there in his final two years of ministry (Mark 6:1-6 and John 7:1-10) on his way to the Feast of Tabernacles. At Jesus' crucifixion, he placed Mary into John's care (John 19:25-27). John would not have left Mary and her family in Jerusalem, at the mercy of the leaders who had Jesus killed. He and the other apostles would have taken the family with them to Galilee. If that is so, Mary would have invited them to stay at her home in Nazareth. They would have set out early the next day on the twenty-mile journey to Capernaum. It would have taken all of Friday, 21/4/30 to walk there.

Thought

The punishment that brought us peace was upon him, and by his wounds we are healed

Day 14

Saturday, 22/4/30

Sabbath celebration in Galilee

Jesus rose to life and appeared to his disciples on Sunday, 9/4/30. The first Sabbath after they saw him was held on Saturday, 15/4/30. The next was held on Saturday, 22/4/30. It was unlawful to walk long distances on Sabbaths, as it was seen as work (Leviticus 23:3). If the disciples left Jerusalem on Monday, 17/4/30 for the five-day walk to Galilee, they would have arrived in Capernaum before the Sabbath began at sunset on Friday, 21/4/30. The day of rest would have given them a chance to recover from the walk to Galilee.

Order of events in Galilee

To set appearances in Galilee on fixed dates, the order they took place needs to be established. John 21:1-23 says Jesus appeared by the lake in Galilee and Matthew 28:16-20 says he appeared on a mountain in Galilee. His lake appearance was his third to his disciples (John 21:14), after the first two in Jerusalem (John 20:19-29). It would have been his first in Galilee and the one on the mountain would have occurred afterwards. Luke 24:49-52 and Acts 3:12 set his next appearances in Jerusalem after they returned from Galilee. The first was when Jesus told them to wait in the city to receive the Holy Spirit and the next was at his ascension from the Mount of Olives.

Day 14 – Saturday, 22/4/30

Besides the appearances recorded in the four Gospels and Acts, five other appearances are recorded in 1 Corinthians 15:5-7. They are:

Jesus' appearances in 1 Corinthians 15:5-7

1. Jesus appeared to Peter
2. Jesus appeared to the Twelve
3. Jesus appeared to more than five hundred brothers
4. Jesus appeared to James
5. Jesus appeared to all the apostles

The Twelve

Jesus appeared to Peter on Resurrection Day (Luke 24:34). When he appeared to the apostles that night, only ten were there, Thomas was absent (John 20:24) and Judas was dead (Matthew 27:3-5). When he appeared to Thomas one week later, eleven apostles were present (John 20:26-29), yet 1 Corinthians 15:5 says he appeared to the Twelve. Jesus appointed twelve apostles: Simon; James; John; Andrew; Philip; Bartholomew; Matthew; Thaddaeus; Thomas, James son of Alphaeus; Simon the zealot; and Judas (Mark 3:16-19) and as he was dead, the original Twelve could not have seen risen Jesus.

Either the apostles were known as the Twelve whether all of them were present or not, or 1 Corinthians 15:5 included Matthias, who replaced Judas as an apostle after the Ascension (Acts 1:15-26). He was there each time Jesus appeared to his disciples (John 20:19-29). If Thomas was absent at his first appearance in the house only eleven apostles, including Matthias were there that night. 1 Corinthians 15:5 cannot refer to that appearance when he said Jesus appeared to the Twelve after appearing to Peter. It must refer to his next appearance to them in the house in Jerusalem on 16/4/30 when all the apostles including Matthias and Thomas were present. It would mean Jesus' other resurrection appearances in 1 Corinthians 15:6-7 happened after he appeared to Thomas on Sunday, 16/4/30.

Day 14 – Saturday, 22/4/30

Appearance to more than five hundred brothers

After appearing to the Twelve, Jesus appeared to over five hundred believers (1 Corinthians 15:6). If the disciples left Jerusalem, the day after Thomas saw Jesus, it is unlikely he appeared to more than five hundred brothers in Jerusalem, before they left for Galilee. If such a large group had gathered there after everyone had left, following the Feast of Unleavened Bread, it would have drawn the attention of the religious leaders who had Jesus killed and the locals who had called for his death. As that fate may have befallen them, it is unlikely he appeared to five hundred brothers gathered in the capital or in one of the towns as the disciples walked to Capernaum (17/4/30 to 21/4/30). The safest place for them to gather was in Galilee away from the jurisdiction of the leaders who had Jesus killed. This would have happened after his (third) appearance by the lake (John 21:14).

Jesus' appearances to all the apostles

1 Corinthians 15:7 says after Jesus appeared to over five hundred believers, he appeared to James then to all the apostles. Jesus appeared to all the apostles three times after his lake appearance:

Jesus' appearances to all the apostles

1. On a mountain in Galilee (Matthew 28:16-20)
2. When Jesus told them to wait in Jerusalem (Acts 1:4-5)
3. At the Ascension from the Mount of Olives (Acts 1:6-12)

Two appearances were in Jerusalem after Jesus' disciples returned from Galilee. If his appearance on a Galilean mountain is not the same as his one to over five hundred brothers (see below), the appearance to 'the Twelve' in 1 Corinthians 15: 7 refers to one of his appearances in Jerusalem. Over five hundred brothers (and James) must have seen Jesus in Galilee after his mountain appearance and before the disciples left Galilee for Jerusalem, as shown below:

Day 14 – Saturday, 22/4/30

Order of Jesus' appearances in Galilee

1. Jesus appeared to Peter and six others by the Sea of Galilee
2. Jesus appeared to his disciples on a Galilean mountain
3. Jesus appeared to more than five hundred brothers
4. Jesus appeared to his brother James

Timeframe of Jesus' appearances in Galilee

Let's see when these events occurred. If the disciples left Jerusalem on Monday 17/4/30, they would have reached Galilee five days later, before the Sabbath began at sunset on Friday, 21/4/30. It ended at sunset on Saturday, 22/4/30. At sunset on Sunday, 23/4/30, a New Moon Festival began and it ended at sunset on Monday, 24/4/30. The nature and duration of Jesus' appearances to his disciples by the lake (John 21:1-23) and on a mountain (Matthew 28:16-20) will determine if they happened in the first few days they were in Galilee.

The appearance by the lake lasted two days. The disciples spent the night of one day fishing and the next day Jesus appeared to them (John 21:1-23). During Jesus' ministry, events on mountains lasted two days. When he chose the apostles, he spent the night in prayer then next day chose the Twelve (Luke 6:12-16). After Jesus fed the Five Thousand, he spent the night praying. Next morning, he walked on water (Mark 6:45-52). Jesus was transfigured on a mountain one day, but it was the next day when he descended it (Luke 9:28-37). If he appeared on one of these mountains, his appearance would have spanned two days. As fishing and walking up and down mountains was unlawful (it was seen as work) on holy days, Jesus could not have appeared by the lake or on a mountain on Saturday, 22/4/30 or Monday, 24/4/30. Neither event could have begun on Friday, 21/4/30 and ended on Saturday, 22/4/30 nor could they have begun on that Sabbath and ended on Sunday, 23/4/30. Likewise – they could not have started that Sunday and ended on Monday, 24/4/30.

Day 14 – Saturday, 22/4/30

The Sabbath celebrated from sunset on Friday, 21/4/30 to sunset on Saturday, 22/4/30 and the New Moon festival held from sunset on Sunday, 23/4/30 to sunset on Monday, 24/4/30 meant Jesus could not have appeared to his disciples by the lake or on a mountain in Galilee from the time they arrived in Galilee before sunset on Friday, 21/4/30 until the New Moon festival ended at sunset on Monday, 24/4/30 as it was unlawful for his apostles to fish or climb up or down mountains on those holy days. The earliest Jesus' appearances in Galilee could have begun was on Tuesday, 25/4/30.

As the disciples witnessed Jesus' ascension from the Mount of Olives on Thursday, 18/5/30, his disciples must have returned from Galilee to Jerusalem by Wednesday, 17/5/30 at the latest. If they walked at twenty miles a day, their walk from Capernaum to the capital would have taken five days. The only unbroken period (when no Sabbath or holy day was celebrated as they travelled) that they could have made their five-day journey to be back in Jerusalem in time to witness the Ascension, was from Sunday, 7/5/30 to Friday, 12/5/30. If that was when they travelled, then Jesus' appearances in Galilee happened from Tuesday, 25/4/30 to Saturday, 6/5/30.

If Jesus' disciples stayed in Galilee from 22/4/30 to 6/5/30, Sabbaths would have been celebrated on 22/4/30; 29/4/30; and 6/5/30, whilst they were there. Also, a New Moon Festival was celebrated on Monday, 24/4/30. These four holy days were days of rest. As they could not fish or climb up and down a Galilean mountain on those days, it meant there were just two unbroken periods during their time in Galilee when Sabbaths and holy days were not celebrated and when these and other appearances in Galilee could have happened:

Timeframe of Jesus' appearances in Galilee

The 4-day period: Tuesday, 25/4/30 to Friday, 28/4/30
The 6-day period: Sunday, 30/4/30 to Friday, 5/5/30

Day 14 – Saturday, 22/4/30

The disciples spent the night of one day fishing and saw Jesus the next day (John 21:1-23). They would have climbed a mountain one day and received the Great Commission (Matthew 28:16-20) then descended it the next day. If Jesus appeared to them on one of the mountains where he prayed before choosing the twelve apostles (Luke 6:12-16) or before he walked on water (Mark 6:45-52), his lake and mountain appearances each lasted two days. If the two appearances did not happen on consecutive days, they could not have occurred in the four-day period, 25/4/30 to 28/4/30.

If Jesus appeared to over five hundred brothers and to James in Galilee and both events happened on separate days (see Appendix) then all four appearances would have lasted a total of six days. If they did not occur on consecutive days they could not have all happened in the six-day period, Sunday, 30/4/30 to Friday, 5/5/30. It would mean Jesus appeared to Peter and six others by the Sea of Galilee in the four-day period, Tuesday, 25/4/30 to Friday, 28/4/30. And he would have appeared to the Eleven on a Galilean mountain in the six-day period, Sunday, 30/4/30 to Friday, 5/5/30.

Sabbath celebration in Galilee

If the disciples arrived in Galilee from Jerusalem on Friday, 21/4/30, they would have arrived before the Sabbath began at sunset. The holy day ended at sunset on Saturday, 22/4/30. It was a day of rest when no work was allowed (Leviticus 23:3). The disciples would have stayed in Capernaum that day. The day of rest would have given them time to recover from their five-day walk from Jerusalem.

Thought

Come to me, all you who are weary and burdened and I will give you rest

Day 15

Sunday, 23/4/30

Monday, 17/4/30, the day after Thomas saw Jesus was the earliest the disciples could have left for Galilee. It was about ninety miles from the capital. If they walked at twenty miles a day, it would have taken five days to get there and they would have arrived on Friday, 21/4/30. Walking long distances was seen as work. It was unlawful on a Sabbath (Leviticus 23:3), so they would have arrived in Galilee before it began at sunset that day. It ended at sunset on Saturday, 22/4/30. The New Moon Festival began twenty-four hours later, at sunset on Sunday, 23/4/30. It celebrated the First Day of the Second Hebrew Month that year and ended it at sunset on Monday, 24/4/30. It was a holy day of rest when work was unlawful. The two days of rest in the first three days after the disciples arrived in Galilee would have affected when Jesus first appeared to them there.

John 21:14 says Jesus' appearance by the lake was his third to his disciples after the first two in Jerusalem (John 20:19-29). It was his first appearance to them in Galilee and spanned two days. On the night of the first day, seven disciples spent the night fishing. Jesus appeared to them the next day and provided a miraculous catch of fish. As fishing was work, this appearance could not have taken place on the Sabbath (22/4/30) and ended on Sunday, 23/4/30 or begun on the Sunday and ended on the New Moon Festival (24/4/30).

Day 15 – Sunday, 23/4/30

Jesus' appearance by the Sea of Galilee could not have happened in the first three days after his disciples arrived in the region, due to the Sabbath celebration on Saturday, 22/4/30 and the New Moon Festival on Monday, 24/4/30. The earliest events of his appearance by the lake could have begun was Tuesday, 25/4/30. If the disciples returned to Jerusalem to witness the Ascension and they travelled in the only possible period when no Sabbath or holy day was held on the way, the journey would have happened in the period, Sunday, 7/5/30 to Friday, 12/5/30. This would mean that Jesus' appearances in Galilee took place from Tuesday, 25/4/30 to Saturday, 6/5/30.

If the disciples arrived in Capernaum before the Sabbath began at sunset on Friday, 21/4/30 and Jesus' first appearance by the Sea of Galilee took place over the two-day period; Tuesday, 25/4/30 to Wednesday, 26/5/30, the disciples would have rested in Capernaum from the time they arrived there (Friday, 21/4/30) until the New Moon Festival ended at sunset on Monday, 24/4/30. Sunday, 23/4/30 would have been one of the days when they remained in Galilee. Three days of rest would have given them time to recover from the five-day walk to Galilee and the emotional rollercoaster they had experienced in Jerusalem witnessing Jesus' death and resurrection.

Thought

Be still and know that I am God

Day 16

Monday, 24/4/30

New Moon celebration in Galilee

If the disciples left Jerusalem the day after Thomas saw Jesus in the house, they would have left on the ninety-odd mile journey to Galilee on Monday, 17/4/30. If they walked at twenty miles a day then they would have arrived in Capernaum five days later on Friday, 21/4/30, before the Sabbath began at sunset. The holy day ended at sunset on Saturday, 22/4/30. It was a day of rest when it was unlawful to work. They would have stayed in Capernaum that day. The day of rest would have given them a chance to recover from the walk to Galilee.

After the Sabbath ended at sunset on Sunday, 23/4/30, the New Moon Festival began. It ended at sunset on Monday 24/4/30. It was a holy day of rest when no work was allowed. The two days of rest in the first three days after the disciples arrived in Galilee affected when Jesus first appeared to them by the lake. The appearance spanned two days. They fished all night one day and he provided a miraculous catch of fish, the next day. As fishing was work, this appearance could not have taken place on the Sabbath celebrated on 22/4/30, which ended twenty-four hours later on Sunday, 23/4/30 or begun on the Sunday and ended on the New Moon Festival (24/4/30).

Day 16 – Monday, 24/4/30

If Jesus' appearance by the Sea of Galilee did not happen from the time the disciples arrived in Galilee before sunset on Friday, 21/4/30 until the New Moon Festival ended at sunset on Monday, 24/4/30, the earliest the events of that appearance could have happened was on Tuesday, 25/4/30. If the disciples returned to Jerusalem in time to witness Jesus' ascension on Thursday, 18/5/30, they would have returned there from Galilee by Wednesday, 17/5/30 at the latest. If they made an unbroken journey from Capernaum to Jerusalem then the only possible period when no Sabbath or holy day was held as they travelled was in the period, Sunday, 7/5/30 to Friday, 12/5/30. It would mean that events in Galilee happened from 25/4/30 to 6/5/30.

If Jesus' lake appearance happened on or after Tuesday, 25/4/30, his disciples would have rested in Capernaum from the time they arrived in Galilee before the Sabbath began at sunset on Friday, 21/4/30 until the New Moon Festival ended at sunset on Monday, 24/4/30. The three days of rest would have given them time to recover from the five-day walk to Galilee and the emotional rollercoaster that they had experienced through witnessing Jesus' death and resurrection.

Monday, 24/4/30 would have been one of the days on which they rested. It was the New Moon Festival. Numbers 28:11-15 says the feast celebrated the rising of the new moon on the first day of every month in the Hebrew calendar. It was the First Day of the Second Hebrew Month. A feast would have been held as it was in the time of King Saul (1 Samuel 20:24-26). Monday, 24/4/30 was a holy day when work, which included walking long distances was unlawful.

Thought

To obey is better than sacrifice

Day 17

Tuesday, 25/4/30

Jesus' disciples spent the night fishing

If the disciples left Jerusalem on Monday, 17/4/30, they would have arrived in Galilee five days later on Friday, 21/4/30. As the Sabbath began at sunset that day, they would have rested in Capernaum until it ended at sunset on Saturday, 22/4/30 (Leviticus 23:3). Twenty-four hours after the Sabbath ended, the New Moon Festival began at sunset on Sunday, 23/4/30. It was a day of rest. The two rest days in the first three days after the disciples returned to Galilee meant the events of Jesus' appearance by the lake that spanned two days could not have occurred in the three-day period, 22/4/30 to 24/4/30.

Timeframe of Jesus' appearances in Galilee

If the disciples returned to Jerusalem from 7/5/30 to 12/5/30, events in Galilee happened from 25/4/30 to 6/5/30. In that time, Sabbaths fell on 29/4/30 and 6/5/30. If the appearances in Galilee did not occur on holy days, there are just two unbroken periods when both of these appearances, each lasting two days could have occurred:

Timeframe of Jesus' appearances in Galilee

The 4-day period: Tuesday, 25/4/30 to Friday, 28/4/30
The 6-day period: Sunday, 30/4/30 to Friday, 5/5/30

Day 17 – Tuesday, 25/4/30

Jesus' appearances by the lake and on a mountain in Galilee each lasted two days. If they did not occur on consecutive days then the two appearances could not have happened in the four-day period, 25/4/30-28/4/30. If his appearance to over five hundred brothers and to James occurred in Galilee on separate days, all four appearances happened over six days. If they did not occur on consecutive days, they did not all occur in the six-day period, 30/4/30-5/5/30. It would mean he appeared by the lake in the four-day period, 25/4/30-28/4/30 and on the mountain in the six-day period, 30/4/30-5/5/30.

Peter fished all night on the Sea of Galilee

The earliest the disciples could have gone fishing was the day after the New Moon Festival ended, Tuesday, 25/4/30. On Resurrection Day, the angel at the tomb and Jesus, told the women from Galilee to tell his disciples he had gone ahead of them to Galilee where they would see him (Matthew 28:5-10). They did not leave Jerusalem for Galilee until the Passover ended and Jesus appeared to Thomas.

In Galilee, it seems Peter grew impatient waiting to see Jesus there. In his desire to do something, he went fishing on the Sea of Galilee. Thomas, Nathaniel, James, John and two other disciples joined him. The seven of them spent the night fishing, but they caught nothing (John 21:1-3). It suggests the disciples did not go fishing under Jesus' authority or in his timing, but their own. Likewise, if we do things in life without Jesus then the results will be fruitless.

Thought

Those who wait on the Lord will never be put to shame

Day 18

Wednesday, 26/4/30

Risen Jesus appeared by the Sea of Galilee

If the disciples spent the night of 25/4/30 fishing, it was the next day when Jesus appeared by the lake and it happened this way:

'Early next day, Jesus stood on the shore, but they did not realise it was him. He called, "Friends, have you any fish?" "No," they replied. He said, "Throw your net on the right side of the boat and you will find some." When they did, they were unable to haul the net in due to the large number of fish. Then the disciple Jesus loved said, "It is the Lord!" When Peter heard him say, "It is the Lord," he wrapped his outer garment around him (for he had taken it off) and jumped in the water. The others followed in the boat, towing the net full of fish. They were not far from shore, about a hundred yards. When they landed, they saw a fire of burning coals there with fish on it, and some bread. Jesus said, "Bring some of the fish you have just caught." Peter climbed aboard and dragged the net ashore. It was full of large fish, 153, but even with so many the net was not torn. He said to them, "Come and have breakfast." None of them dared ask him, "Who are you?" They knew it was the Lord. Jesus came, took the bread and gave it to them, and did the same with the fish. It was now the third time he had appeared to them after he was raised to life.

Day 18 – Wednesday, 26/4/30

When they had finished eating, Jesus said to Simon, "Simon, son of John, do you truly love me more than these?" "Yes, Lord," he said, "you know that I love you." Jesus said, "Feed my lambs." Again Jesus said, "Simon, son of John, do you truly love me?" He answered "Yes, Lord, you know that I love you." Jesus said, "Take care of my sheep." The third time he said to him, "Simon, son of John, do you love me?" Peter was hurt because Jesus asked him the third time, "Do you love me?" He said, "Lord, you know all things; you know that I love you." Jesus said, "Feed my sheep. I tell you the truth, when you were younger you dressed yourself and went where you wanted; but when you are old you will stretch out your hands, someone else will dress you and lead you where you do not want to go. He said this to indicate the kind of death by which Peter would glorify God. Then he said to him, "Follow me!" Peter turned and saw the disciple whom Jesus loved was following them (this was the one who leaned back against Jesus at the supper and had said, "Lord, who is going to betray you?"). When Peter saw John, he asked, "Lord, what about him?" Jesus answered, "If I want him to remain alive until I return, what is that to you? You must follow me!" (John 21:4-23).

The account of this appearance by the lake in John 21:4-23 reveals the event happened over two days. Peter and six others spent the night of one day fishing and caught nothing. It was in the morning of the next day when Jesus appeared to them on the shore. The first time Jesus appeared to them by the Sea of Galilee (when he called them to be disciples), he provided a miracle catch of fish that was so big their nets almost broke and their boats almost sank (Luke 5:1-7). This time, the catch was so big, they were unable to haul the net in (John 21:6). Each time Jesus showed the abundance of his provision. When they came ashore he supplied their immediate need and fed them breakfast. If the disciples spent the night of Tuesday, 25/4/30 fishing on the Sea of Galilee, then Jesus would have appeared to them early in the morning of Wednesday, 26/4/30.

Day 18 – Wednesday, 26/4/30

Jesus re-instated Peter in his ministry

When Peter came ashore, he saw Jesus standing by a fire of burning coals. The last time he had seen a fire of burning coals was the night he denied Jesus three times. After breakfast, he asked Peter three times if he loved him (the same number of times he had denied him). Each time he said, 'Yes!' Then Jesus re-instated him in his ministry to look after his sheep. Peter had failed badly. On the way to Gethsemane, Jesus said his disciples would desert him. Peter said if the others fell away he would not. He was trusting in his own love for Jesus to see him through. Jesus said he would betray him before the cock crowed (Mark 14:27-31). That night he deserted Jesus (Mark 14:50) then denied him three times (Mark 14:66-72).

Yet, on Resurrection Day, the angel at the tomb told the women to tell the disciples and Peter Jesus is risen and they would see him in Galilee (Mark 16:6-7). Even though he had messed up, he was still on God's heart to receive a special mention. How reassuring it must have been to know that. God's love was shown again that day when Jesus appeared to Peter personally (1 Corinthians 15:3-5 and Luke 24:34). The events of that appearance were not recorded, but it is clear Jesus restored Peter emotionally at that time. It is such an encouragement to us. We have all messed up. The good news is, it does not stop God loving us and finding ways to restore us.

Peter was unable to recognise Jesus standing on the shore. When he provided a miraculous catch of fish, it was John not Peter, who was the first to see it was Jesus. It reveals a big difference between Peter and John. On the night he betrayed Jesus, Peter trusted in his own love for Jesus, *"If all fall away. I will not"* (Mark 14:29). John on the other hand, who referred to himself as, *'the disciple whom Jesus loved'* (John 13:23), trusted in Jesus' love for him. And it was John who was first to recognise his risen Lord beside the Sea of Galilee.

Day 18 – Wednesday, 26/4/30

This appearance reveals a huge growth in Peter's faith. When John said it was Jesus on the shore, he leapt out of the boat and hurried to him. The first time he provided a miracle catch of fish, Peter begged Jesus to leave him because of his sinfulness (Luke 5:1-11). That time, he recognised Jesus' holiness and his own sinfulness. It made him want Jesus to go away. This time he recognised and accepted Jesus' love for him. It made him run to him. Peter saw Jesus loved him and accepted him, despite all his shortcomings. God never withdraws his love because we sin or fall. We are always acceptable to Him and His arms are always open wide to embrace us. When we believe He loves us and believe Jesus died for us we will always run into our heavenly Father's open arms when we sin or fall.

Peter saw Jesus standing by a fire of burning coals. The last time he saw him and a fire of burning coals was the night he betrayed him. Now he saw Jesus alive, standing by a fire. He who had suffered and died was now alive forever. What a joyous sight for Peter to behold. Jesus took this bad memory for Peter and turned it into a wonderful one. What love Jesus showed and he will do the same for us. He will take the worst things that have ever happened in our lives and turn them into the best things that ever happened, if we will let him.

Risen Jesus appeared to Peter most times

How reassuring it must have been for Peter that over the forty days of resurrection appearances, it was he, who abandoned his Lord and denied knowing him three times was the one Jesus appeared to most. The leader of Christ's Church saw risen Jesus eight times.

Thought

Come to me, all you who are weary and burdened and I will give you rest

Day 19

Thursday, 27/4/30

Jesus' disciples stayed in Galilee

If the disciples left Jerusalem on the five-day walk to Galilee on Monday, 17/4/30 (after Thomas saw Jesus), they would have arrived before the Sabbath began at sunset on Friday, 21/4/30. The holy day of rest (Leviticus 23:3) ended at sunset on Saturday, 22/4/30. Monday, 24/4/30 was a New Moon Festival. It was unlawful to work that day. The lake appearance (John 21:1-23) lasted two days. It involved fishing each day. At the appearance on a mountain in Galilee (Matthew 28:16-20), the Eleven climbed the mountain one day and descended it the next. Climbing mountains and fishing were seen as work and were unlawful on those holy days. So Jesus' appearances could not have happened until both holy days ended. The earliest his appearances in Galilee could have begun was 25/4/30.

For the disciples to witness the Ascension from the Mount of Olives on Thursday, 18/5/30, they must have returned to Jerusalem by Wednesday, 17/5/30 at the latest. The latest unbroken period (when no holy day was held as they travelled) they could have made the five-day walk to be in Jerusalem to see the Ascension, was from Sunday, 7/5/30 to Friday, 12/5/30. It means Jesus' appearances in Galilee happened from Tuesday, 25/4/30 to Saturday, 6/5/30.

Day 19 – Thursday, 27/4/30

If Jesus' disciples arrived in Galilee on Friday, 21/4/30 and they left on Sunday, 7/5/30; three Sabbath were held in that timeframe; on 22/4/30; 29/4/30; and 6/5/30 and a New Moon Festival was held on 24/4/30. The holy days of rest meant the disciples could not have fished on the lake or climbed up and down a mountain in Galilee on those days. It left just two unbroken timeframes during the disciples' time in Galilee when Jesus' appearances could have occurred:

Timeframe of Jesus' appearances in Galilee

The 4-day period: Tuesday, 25/4/30 to Friday, 28/4/30
The 6-day period: Sunday, 30/4/30 to Friday, 5/5/30

Jesus' lake and mountain appearances each lasted two days. If they did not occur on consecutive days, both could not have happened in the four-day period, 25/4/30 to 28/4/30. If Jesus' appearances to over five hundred brothers and to James recorded in 1 Corinthians 15:6-7 took place in Galilee on separate days (see Appendix) then all four appearances would have lasted a total of six days. If they did not occur on consecutive days they could not have all happened in the six-day period, 30/4/30-5/5/30. Jesus must have appeared by the lake in the four-day period, 25/4/30-28/4/30 then on a Galilean mountain and to more than five hundred brothers and to James in the six-day period, 30/4/30-5/5/30. If Jesus' appearance by the Sea of Galilee happened from Tuesday, 25/4/30 to Wednesday, 26/4/30 and he did not appear on a Galilean mountain until 30/4/30 at the earliest, his disciples would have stayed in Galilee from 27/4/30 to 29/4/30. Thursday, 27/4/30 would have been one of those days when they stayed in Capernaum.

Thought

I will give you rest

Day 20

Friday, 28/4/30

Jesus' disciples stayed in Galilee

If the disciples travelled to Galilee (after Jesus appeared to Thomas) from 17/4/30 to 21/4/30, two holy days were held in the first three days after they arrived. A Sabbath was held from sunset on Friday, 21/4/30 to sunset on Saturday, 22/4/30 and the New Moon Festival was held from Sunday, 23/4/30 to Monday, 24/4/30. They were days of rest when no work was allowed. The appearance by the lake lasted two days and his disciples fished on both days (John 21:1-23). At the appearance on a Galilean mountain (Matthew 28:16-20), they climbed the mountain one day and descended it the next. As fishing and climbing mountains was seen as work, both appearances could not have occurred in the three days after they arrived in Galilee.

John 21:14 says that Jesus' appearance by the Sea of Galilee was his third to his disciples. As the first two were in the house in Jerusalem (John 20:19-29), this appearance would have been his first in Galilee. As Jesus' disciples fished on both days and fishing was work, this appearance could not have taken place from the time they arrived in Galilee on Friday, 21/4/30 to Monday, 24/4/30. The earliest Jesus could have appeared to his disciples by the lake was over the two-day period, Tuesday, 25/4/30 to Wednesday, 26/4/30.

Day 20 – Friday, 28/4/30

If the disciples witnessed Jesus' ascension at the Mount of Olives on Thursday, 18/5/30, they must have returned to Jerusalem by 17/5/30 at the latest. The only unbroken period (when no Sabbath fell on the way) they could have returned from Galilee was from Sunday, 7/5/30 to Friday, 12/5/30. If they arrived in Galilee on 21/4/30 and left on 7/5/30, Sabbaths were held in that period on 22/4/30; 29/4/30; and 6/5/30; and a New Moon Festival was held on 24/4/30. These rest days meant they could not fish or climb up and down a mountain on those days. It leaves two unbroken periods during their time in Galilee when these appearances could have occurred:

Timeframe of Jesus' appearances in Galilee

The 4-day period: Tuesday, 25/4/30 to Friday, 28/4/30
The 6-day period: Sunday, 30/4/30 to Friday, 5/5/30

Jesus' lake and mountain appearances each lasted two days. If they did not occur on consecutive days, both did not happen in the four-day period, 25/4/30-28/4/30. If he appeared by the lake from 25/4/30 to 26/4/30; the earliest he could have appeared on a mountain was Friday, 28/4/30. If the disciples ascended the mountain then they could not have descended it the next day as it was a Sabbath when no work, which included climbing mountains was allowed. So they could not have climbed the mountain on the Sabbath and descended it the next day (Sunday, 30/4/30). The earliest this appearance could have occurred is in the six-day period, 30/4/30 to 5/5/30, beginning on Sunday, 30/4/30. It would mean the disciples stayed in Galilee after Jesus' appearance by the lake to the day before he appeared on the mountain (Thursday, 27/4/30 to Saturday, 29/4/30). Friday, 28/4/30 would have been one of the days they stayed in Galilee.

Thought

Be still and wait on God

Day 21

Saturday, 29/4/30

Sabbath celebration in Galilee

If the disciples made unbroken journeys (when no Sabbaths or holy days were held as they travelled) from Jerusalem to Galilee and from there back to the capital, the only time they could have occurred was from 17/4/30 to 21/4/30 and from 7/5/30 to 12/5/30. During their time in Galilee (22/4/30-6/5/30), Sabbaths would have been celebrated on 22/4/30; 29/4/30 and 6/5/30, and a New Moon Festival was held on Monday, 14/4/30. The timing of these holy days of rest meant Jesus' appearances in Galilee happened in two unbroken periods of time:

Timeframe of Jesus' appearances in Galilee

The 4-day period: Tuesday, 25/4/30 to Friday, 28/4/30
The 6-day period: Sunday, 30/4/30 to Friday, 5/5/30

If Jesus' appearances by the lake and on a mountain in Galilee each lasted two days, and they did not happen on consecutive days, they could not have happened in the four-day period, 25/4/30 to 28/4/30. John 21:14 says Jesus' appearance by the Sea of Galilee was his third to his disciples. His first two were in Jerusalem (John 20:19-29). It would have been his first to them in Galilee and would have happened in the four-day period, 25/4/30 to 28/4/30.

67

Day 21 – Saturday, 29/4/30

The earliest Jesus' lake appearance could have happened was on Tuesday, 25/4/30 to Wednesday, 26/4/30. If his next appearance was on a mountain in Galilee, it did not occur on Thursday, 27/4/30, if the two appearances did not happen on consecutive days.

Events on mountains during his time of ministry spanned two days. When Jesus chose the apostles, he went up a mountain one day and spent the night praying. In the morning of the next day he chose the Twelve (Luke 6:12-16). After he fed the Five Thousand, he went up a mountain. He prayed from sunset of that day until the fourth watch of the night, which began at 03:00 Hours the next day. Then he walked on the Sea of Galilee (Mark 6:45-52). At his transfiguration, Jesus went up the mountain one day with Peter, James and John and was transfigured. It was the next day when they came down the mountain (Luke 9:28-37). Each time, they stayed on the mountain overnight. There may not have been enough daylight remaining for the disciples to descend the mountain safely. If it was on one of these mountains that Jesus appeared to the Eleven, then it happened over two days.

Ascending and descending mountains was seen as work and was unlawful on a Sabbath (Exodus 20:8-11). Jesus' disciples could not have ascended or descended a mountain in Galilee to receive the Great Commission on Saturday, 29/4/30 as it was a day of rest. The earliest this two-day appearance on a Galilean mountain could have begun was the next day, Sunday, 30/4/30 and it would have ended on Monday, 1/5/30. Jesus' disciples would have spent the Sabbath, Saturday, 29/4/30 resting in Capernaum in Galilee.

Thought

We proclaim to you what we have seen and heard, so you also may have fellowship with us

Day 22

Sunday, 30/4/30

Jesus appeared on a Galilean mountain

If Jesus' disciples left Jerusalem on Monday, 17/4/30, the day after he appeared to Thomas, the earliest they could have arrived in Galilee after a five-day walk there would have been Friday, 21/4/30. The Sabbath began at sunset that day and ended twenty-four hours later at sunset on Saturday, 22/4/30. Then a New Moon Festival was held from sunset on Sunday, 23/4/30 to sunset on Monday, 24/4/30. Jesus' first appearance by the lake happened over two days. The disciples spent the night of one day fishing and the next morning, Jesus provided them with a miraculous catch of fish. As they fished on both days, this event could not have happened in the first three days they were in Galilee as it was unlawful to work on holy days in Israel.

The earliest the event could have begun was the day after the New Moon Festival ended. Peter and six others would have spent the night of Tuesday, 25/4/30 fishing on the Sea of Galilee and caught nothing. It would have been the morning of Wednesday, 26/4/30 when Jesus appeared to them on the shore and provided them with a miraculous catch of fish and re-instated Peter in his ministry (John 21:1-23). If his lake and mountain appearances did not happen on consecutive days then Jesus did not appear on a mountain on Thursday, 27/4/30.

Day 22 – Sunday, 30/4/30

If Jesus appeared to his disciples on the mountain where he chose the apostles (Luke 6:12-16) or on the one where he prayed before walking on water (Mark 6:45-52) or on the Mount of Transfiguration (Luke 9:28-37), this appearance would also have lasted two days. They would have climbed the mountain one day and descended it the next. They could not have ascended it on Friday, 28/4/30 as the next day, 29/4/30 was a Sabbath. Descending mountains was seen as work and was unlawful on a Sabbath (Leviticus 23:3). Also, this two-day appearance could not have begun on Saturday, 29/4/30 and ended the next day, Sunday, 30/4/30 as it would have been unlawful to climb the mountain on a Sabbath. The earliest this appearance could have happened was Sunday, 30/4/30 to Monday, 1/5/30.

On Resurrection Day, when Jesus told the women at the tomb to tell his disciples to go to Galilee where they would see him, he did not say when or where (Matthew 28:8-10). Yet Matthew 28:16 says they went to the mountain where he had told them to go. If they did not receive this information in Jerusalem; he must have told the disciples when and where at his lake appearance on Wednesday, 26/4/30.

At his mountain appearance, Jesus was worshipped, but some doubted (Matthew 28:17). It is unlikely any apostle doubted. It was the fourth time most of them had seen him after his resurrection: twice in the capital (John 20:19-29); and once by the lake (John 21:1-23). If none of the Eleven doubted, there must have been others on the mountain who did. Let's see if the Gospels reveal who the others were. On Resurrection Day when the women returned to the house, they told the Eleven and all the others everything they had witnessed at the tomb (Luke 24:9). After the two disciples had seen Jesus at Emmaus, they ran to the house in Jerusalem, where they found the Eleven and those with them assembled together (Luke 24:33). These verses show that there were other believers with the disciples in the house on the day Jesus rose from the dead.

Day 22 – Sunday, 30/4/30

Acts 1:13-15 says after Jesus' ascension from the Mount of Olives; the Eleven returned to the house in Jerusalem. There they prayed with the women, Mary from Galilee, Jesus' mother and his brothers. Then Peter addressed the group of about a hundred and twenty disciples. If they were *all the others'* in the house with the Eleven on Resurrection Day when the women and the two disciples from Emmaus said they had seen Jesus, they too would have received the instruction to go to Galilee to see him. It is unlikely such a large number of disciples stayed in Jerusalem where the religious leaders conspired to have Jesus killed and the locals called for his blood. They would have gone to Galilee with the apostles. If they were on the mountain, it would have been some of them who doubted.

Is it possible Jesus' appearance on the mountain could have been his one to over five hundred brothers (1 Corinthians 15:6) and some of them doubted? Act 2:1-7 says at Pentecost, they were all in one place when they were filled with the Spirit and they were all Galileans. The 'all' refers to the Eleven and the hundred and twenty believers recorded in Acts 1:12-26, in the house after the Ascension. So the hundred and twenty were there on Resurrection Day; Ascension Day; and Pentecost and they were all Galilean (Acts 2:7). As they were in the house on Resurrection Day (Luke 24:9-10), they would have heard the order to go to Galilee to see Jesus (Mark 16:6-7). They would have gone there with the Eleven. As they did not see Jesus by the Sea of Galilee, some of them may have doubted on the mountain.

When Jesus appeared to his disciples on the mountain in Galilee, he gave them the Great Commission to make disciples of all nations, beginning in Jerusalem (Matthew 28:16-20). As the hundred and twenty were with the Eleven at the Ascension and at Pentecost, it suggests it was they who received the Great Commission that day, and it was they who returned to Jerusalem with the Eleven to be empowered by the Holy Spirit to carry out that Great Commission.

Day 22 – Sunday, 30/4/30

If it had been the more than five hundred brothers who had received the Great Commission on the Galilean mountain, it would have been they who returned to Jerusalem with the apostles, and it would have been they who were in the house with them after the Ascension. And it would have been the more than five hundred brothers who were baptised with the Holy Spirit at Pentecost. However, the Scriptures say it was the hundred and twenty believers who were in the house after the Ascension and at Pentecost. If the more than five hundred believers were present at the appearance on a Galilean mountain, it would mean over three hundred and eighty of them refused to take up the Great Commission to make disciples of all nations and did not go to Jerusalem to begin that work. It is highly unlikely such a large number of believers would have refused Jesus' Great Commission.

It would mean Jesus' appearance on the mountain in Galilee and his appearance to more than five hundred brothers at the same time are two separate events. It may have been after the hundred and twenty believers came down the mountain; they put the Great Commission into practise and gathered a large group of brothers together to tell them they had seen Jesus resurrected from the dead. It would have been when they were all together that he appeared to them. If Jesus appeared on the mountain on Sunday, 30/4/30, he would have given the Great Commission to make disciples of all nations that day.

Thought

Go and make disciples of all nations baptising them in the name of the Father and of the Son and of the Holy Spirit, and teaching them to obey everything I have commanded you

Day 23

Monday, 1/5/30

Jesus' disciples descended the mountain

If Jesus' disciples walked to Galilee the day after he had appeared to Thomas in Jerusalem on Sunday, 16/4/30, they would have arrived there five days later on Friday, 21/4/30. Due to the Sabbath held on Saturday, 22/4/30 and the New Moon Festival on Monday, 24/4/30, Jesus' first appearance there by the lake, which happened over two days could not have begun until the holy days ended. So the earliest his appearances in Galilee could have begun was Tuesday, 25/4/30. If the only unbroken period (when no Sabbath fell on the way) they could have returned to Jerusalem was from 7/5/30 to 12/5/30, it would mean appearances in Galilee occurred from 25/4/30 to 6/5/30,

Owing to the Sabbaths held on 29/4/30 and 6/5/30, events in Galilee could have occurred only in two unbroken periods of time: Tuesday, 25/4/30 to Friday, 28/4/30 and Sunday, 30/4/30 to Friday, 5/5/30. If Jesus' appearances by the lake and on a mountain each lasted two days, and they did not happen on consecutive days, both could not have occurred in the four-day period, 25/4/30 to 28/4/30. Jesus' lake appearance was his third to his disciples (John 21:14) and his first to them in Galilee. It would have taken place in the four-day period, 25/4/30 to 28/4/30 – from Tuesday, 25/4/30 to Wednesday, 26/4/30.

Day 23 – Monday, 1/5/30

If Jesus' appearances by the lake and on a mountain in Galilee did not occur on consecutive days then he did not appear on a mountain on Thursday, 27/4/30. If his disciples climbed the mountain in Galilee and received the Great Commission one day then descended the slopes the next day, the appearance could not have begun on Friday, 28/4/30 and ended on Saturday, 29/4/30 as they would have descended the mountain on the Sabbath, which was unlawful (Leviticus 23:3). Also, they could not have ascended the mountain on the Sabbath (29/4/30) to see Jesus and descended it the next day (30/4/30). After his lake appearance, the earliest Jesus could have appeared on a Galilean mountain was Sunday, 30/4/30.

Events on mountains during Jesus' time of ministry spanned two days. When he chose the apostles (Luke 6:12-16); when he walked on water (Mark 6:45-52); and at his transfiguration (Luke 9:28-37). Each time, he stayed on the mountain overnight. If Jesus appeared on one of those mountains, it would have happened over two days. If it was not the same appearance as his one to more than five hundred brothers and it happened on Sunday, 30/4/30, his disciples would have climbed the mountain and seen Jesus that day.

Though some of those on the mountain doubted, it did not stop the Lord giving them the Great Commission to make disciples of all nations. The disciples would have spent that Sunday night on the mountain. There would not have been enough time to climb down the mountain safely before darkness fell. If the disciples slept on the mountain overnight, they would have descended its slopes first thing the next day, which was Monday, 1/5/30.

Thought

This is my Son, whom I love. Listen to him!

Day 24

Tuesday, 2/5/30

Jesus' disciples stayed in Galilee

If the Eleven walked to Galilee from 17/4/30 to 21/4/30 and returned to Jerusalem from 7/5/30 to 12/5/30, events in Galilee happened from 22/4/30 to 6/5/30. The Sabbaths held on 22/4/30; 29/4/30 and 6/5/30 and the New Moon Festival on 24/4/30 mean there are two unbroken periods when Jesus' appearances in Galilee could have occurred:

Timeframe of Jesus' appearances in Galilee

The 4-day period: Tuesday, 25/4/30 to Friday, 28/4/30
The 6-day period: Sunday, 30/4/30 to Friday, 5/5/30

Jesus' appearances by the lake and on a mountain in Galilee each lasted two days. If they did not occur on consecutive days, both could not have occurred in the four-day period, 25/4/30 to 28/4/30. If Jesus' appearance to more than five hundred brothers and to his brother James (1 Corinthians 15:6-7) took place in Galilee on separate days, it would mean all four appearances lasted six days. If they did not occur on consecutive days, they could not have all happened in the six-day period, 30/4/30 to 5/5/30. The lake appearance would have happened from 25/4/30 to 28/4/30 and the other three appearances would have taken place from Sunday, 30/4/30 to Friday, 5/5/30.

Day 24 – Tuesday, 2/5/30

To confirm the order and chronology of Jesus' Galilean appearances, it is necessary to examine his appearances in 1 Corinthians 15:5-7 alongside those recorded in the Gospels.

Resurrection appearances in 1 Corinthians 15:5-7

1. Jesus appeared to Peter
2. Then Jesus appeared to the Twelve
3. After that Jesus was seen by over five hundred brothers
4. Then Jesus appeared to his brother James
5. Then Jesus appeared to all the apostles

Jesus appeared to Peter and to the Twelve in Jerusalem before they went to Galilee (Luke 24:34 and John 20:26-29). His appearances to over five hundred brothers; to James then to all of the apostles would have occurred after they left for Galilee on Monday, 17/4/30 and before the Ascension from the Mount of Olives on Thursday, 18/5/30. It is unlikely he was seen by over five hundred brothers as the apostles walked to Galilee (17/4/30-21/4/30) or as they returned to Jerusalem (7/5/30-12/5/30) or whilst they were in the city before the Ascension (13/5/30-18/5/30). If such a big group of disciples had gathered in a town as they travelled or in the capital, it would have drawn unwarranted attention and put their lives at risk. The safest place for them to gather in such large numbers would have been in Galilee, away from those who had orchestrated Jesus' death.

If over five hundred brothers saw Jesus in Galilee, it would have been after he appeared by the lake on Wednesday, 26/4/30 as that was his third to his disciples (John 21:14). If they had seen him before that, John would have said the lake appearance was his fourth. To find when over five hundred disciples, and James saw him we need to examine when he appeared to all the apostles (1 Corinthians 15:7). The Gospels say Jesus appeared to them three times after he appeared to Peter and the other disciples by the Sea of Galilee.

Day 24 – Tuesday, 2/5/30

When Jesus appeared to all the apostles

1. Jesus appeared to his disciples on a mountain in Galilee
2. When he told the Eleven to stay in the city to receive the Spirit
3. At the Ascension from the Mount of Olives

Timeframe if they all saw Jesus on a mountain

If Jesus' appearance to all the apostles is the same as his mountain appearance (Matthew 28:16-20), he was seen by over five hundred brothers and James on separate occasions, prior to his mountain appearance and after his lake appearance, as shown below:

Timeframe if they all saw Jesus on a mountain

1. Jesus appeared to seven disciples by the Sea of Galilee
2. Jesus appeared to more than five hundred brothers
3. Jesus appeared to his brother James
4. Jesus appeared to his disciples on a mountain in Galilee

Timeframe if they all saw Jesus in Jerusalem

If the appearance to all the apostles refers to one of Jesus' final two appearances in Jerusalem then events in Galilee occurred this way:

Timeframe if they all saw Jesus in Jerusalem

1. Jesus appeared to seven disciples by the Sea of Galilee
2. Jesus appeared to his disciples on a mountain in Galilee
3. Jesus appeared to more than five hundred brothers
4. Jesus appeared to his brother James

It was shown, it was the hundred and twenty disciples who were with the apostles in the house on Resurrection Day, Ascension Day and at Pentecost (Acts 1:12-2:7). It was they and not the five hundred plus brothers who received Jesus' Great Commission on a mountain and returned to Jerusalem to receive the Holy Spirit to carry it out.

Day 24 – Tuesday, 2/5/30

If the appearance on a Galilean mountain and the one to over five hundred believers occurred on separate occasions, the mountain appearance would have happened first. Then after he appeared to more than five hundred brothers at the same time, he appeared to James. If Jesus' disciples received the Great Commission from Sunday, 30/4/30 to Monday, 1/5/30 then he would have been seen by over five hundred brothers at the same time, and by his brother James from the day after his mountain appearance to the day his disciples left Galilee (Tuesday, 2/5/30 to Sunday, 7/5/30). If these appearances did not happen on consecutive days, Jesus could not have appeared to more than five hundred brothers on the day after he appeared to the Eleven on a mountain in Galilee. So this appearance could not have happened on Tuesday, 2/5/30. It would have been one of the days that Jesus' disciples remained in Galilee.

If Jesus appeared on a mountain on 30/4/30, then the disciples would have descended the slope on 1/5/30. It appears they put the command to share the good news of his resurrection into practise as they soon assembled over five hundred believers. Whilst they were together Jesus appeared to them all (1 Corinthians 15:6). It would have taken time for those who saw him on the mountain to assemble a group of over five hundred believers. Tuesday, 2/5/30 would have been one of the days they went around telling people the good news Jesus had died for their sins and had risen to life victorious over death and they had seen him alive on a Galilean mountain.

Thought

I tell you, whoever acknowledges me before men, I will acknowledge him before my Father in heaven

Day 25

Wednesday, 3/5/30

Jesus appeared to over five hundred brothers

If the disciples travelled from to Galilee from Monday, 17/4/30 to Friday, 21/4/30 and returned to Jerusalem from Sunday, 7/5/30 to Friday, 12/5/30, events there occurred from Saturday, 22/4/30 to Saturday, 6/5/30. If Jesus' appearances in Galilee did not happen on holy days, there are only two unbroken periods when his appearances to his disciples in Galilee could have taken place:

Timeframe of Jesus' appearances in Galilee

The 4-day period: Tuesday, 25/4/30 to Friday, 28/4/30
The 6-day period: Sunday, 30/4/30 to Friday, 5/5/30

Jesus' lake and mountain appearances in Galilee each lasted two days. If both appearances did not occur on consecutive days, they could not have happened in the four-day period, 25/4/30 to 28/4/30. If he was seen by over five hundred brothers and by James in Galilee on separate days after his mountain appearance, it means he appeared by the lake in the four-day period, Monday, 25/4/30 to Friday, 28/4/30 and his other three appearances in Galilee occurred in the six-day period, Sunday, 30/4/30 to Friday, 5/5/30.

Day 25 – Wednesday, 3/5/30

The earliest Jesus could have appeared on a mountain in Galilee in the six-day period, 30/4/30-5/5/30 was on Sunday, 30/4/30. If Jesus gave his disciples the Great Commission that day, they would have stayed on the mountain overnight and descended it the next day, Monday, 1/5/30. Jesus' next appearance was to over five hundred brothers (1 Corinthians 15:6). If the two appearances did not occur on consecutive days then Jesus could not have been seen by more than five hundred believers on Tuesday, 2/5/30. It seems that from the time the disciples descended the mountain on 1/5/30, they put the Great Commission into practise and shared with others that Jesus had died and risen again and had appeared to them.

If he was not seen by over five hundred brothers on Tuesday, 2/5/30 then the disciples would have spent that day testifying Jesus was the Christ and had risen from the dead. The more they witnessed, the more the number of believers grew. The group continued to grow on Wednesday, 3/5/30 until the numbers gathered around the disciples had increased to more than five hundred. Whilst they were together, Jesus appeared to all of them, including the eleven apostles and the hundred and twenty disciples who saw him on the mountain.

Thought

So Jesus is not ashamed to call them brothers

Day 26

Thursday, 4/5/30

Jesus' disciples stayed in Galilee

If the disciples walked from Jerusalem to Galilee from 17/4/30 to 21/4/30 and returned there from 7/5/30 to 12/5/30; appearances in Galilee would have occurred from 22/4/30 to 6/5/30. If they did not occur on holy days, they would have occurred either in the four-day period, 25/4/30-28/4/30 or in the six-day period, 30/4/30-5/5/30.

If his lake and mountain appearances lasted two days and did not occur on consecutive days, both did not happen in the four-day period, 25/4/30 to 28/4/30. If Jesus appeared to over five hundred brothers and James in Galilee on separate days after his mountain appearance, his lake appearance happened in the four-day period, 25/4/30-28/4/30 and his other appearances from 30/4/30 to 5/5/30.

The earliest his disciples could have seen Jesus on the mountain was Sunday, 30/4/30. After receiving the Great Commission, they would have stayed on the mountain overnight and descended it the next day, Monday, 1/5/30. If his appearance on a mountain and to more than five hundred believers did not happen consecutively then Jesus could not have been seen by more than five hundred brothers at the same time on the following day, Tuesday, 2/5/30.

Day 26 – Thursday, 4/5/30

After the disciples saw Jesus and received the Great Commission, they descended the mountain on Monday, 1/5/30. From that time it seems, they shared with others they had seen Jesus alive after he was crucified and buried. They would have continued to testify that Jesus had risen from the dead on Tuesday, 2/5/30.

It seems the number of believers that gathered around them continued to increase as they shared the good news about Jesus' death and resurrection on Wednesday, 3/5/30. When more than five hundred of them had gathered together, risen Jesus appeared to them all at the same time. This group would have included the eleven apostles and the hundred and twenty disciples who had witnessed Jesus' appearance on the mountain in Galilee.

If the appearance to over five hundred believers at the same time and the appearance to James did not happen on consecutive days, Jesus could not have been seen by his brother on Thursday, 4/5/30. On that day, his disciples would have remained in Galilee.

Thought

Those closest to us can take longest to respond to God's loving offer in Christ Jesus

Day 27

Friday, 5/5/30

Risen Jesus appeared to James

If the disciples travelled to Galilee from 17/4/30 to 21/4/30 and they returned to Jerusalem from 7/5/30 to 12/5/30, his appearances there would have occurred from 22/4/30 to 6/5/30. If they did not occur on Sabbaths and holy days, they occurred in these periods:

Timeframe of Jesus' appearances in Galilee

The 4-day period: Tuesday, 25/4/30 to Friday, 28/4/30
The 6-day period: Sunday, 30/4/30 to Friday, 5/5/30

If Jesus' lake and mountain appearances each lasted two days and did not occur on consecutive days, both did not occur from 25/4/30 to 28/4/30. If he was seen by over five hundred brothers and James on separate days after his mountain appearance then he appeared by the lake in the four-day period, 25/4/30-28/4/30 and his other appearances occurred in the six-day period, 30/4/30-5/5/30. The earliest his disciples could have seen Jesus on the mountain in that period was Sunday, 30/4/30. They would have descended it the next day (Monday, 1/5/30). It seems they put the Great Commission into practise right away and the number of believers increased to over five hundred and Jesus appeared to them all on Wednesday, 3/5/30.

Day 27 – Friday, 5/5/30

If Jesus' appearances to over five hundred brothers and to James did not happen on consecutive days, James did not see him on Thursday, 4/5/30. If he did not appear to his disciples on holy days, he would not have been seen by James on Saturday, 6/5/30. If the disciples left Galilee on Sunday, 7/5/30 to return to Jerusalem, it would mean, the only day he could have appeared to his brother (if he appeared to him in Galilee) was on Friday, 5/5/30.

As he bled and died for the sins of the world on the cross, Jesus committed Mary into the care of his disciple, John (John 19:25-27). John and the other disciples would have taken Mary and Jesus' siblings with them when they returned to Galilee. They would not have left Jesus' family in Jerusalem at the mercy of the religious leaders who had orchestrated his death or the residents of the city who had called for his blood. The Lord's family would have stayed in Galilee with the disciples until they returned to Jerusalem.

Mary and Jesus' brothers were with the disciples in the house in Jerusalem after he ascended into heaven and his family joined the apostles in prayer (Acts 1:12-14). It implies they witnessed Jesus ascend into heaven and believed he was the Son of God, who is God, who died for the sins of the world and rose again on third day. James had come to believe in Jesus' deity from the time he teased him in his final year of ministry (John 7:2-9) and his ascension. James' conversion may have happened when Jesus appeared to him alone in his resurrected form on Friday, 5/5/30.

Thought

For this son of mine was dead and is alive again; he was lost and is found

Day 28

Saturday, 6/5/30

Sabbath celebration in Galilee

If after Jesus rose from the dead, his disciples travelled to Galilee from 17/4/30 to 21/4/30 and they returned to Jerusalem from 7/5/30 to 12/5/30, he would have appeared to them in Galilee from 22/4/30 to 6/5/30. If Jesus did not appear to them on Sabbaths or holy days, they would have seen him in the four-day period, 25/4/30-28/4/30 or in the six-day period, 30/4/30-5/5/30.

If Jesus' appearances did not happen consecutively, his two-day appearances by the lake and on a Galilean mountain could not have occurred in the four-day period, 25/4/30-28/4/30. His appearance by the lake would have taken place in that timeframe, from 25/4/30 to 26/4/30. And he would have appeared on a mountain; to over five hundred brothers, and to James in the six-day period, 30/4/30 to 5/5/30. The earliest his disciples could have seen him on a mountain was Sunday, 30/4/30. After receiving the Great Commission, they descended the mountain the next day and put it into practise until Wednesday, 3/5/30. A crowd of over five hundred brothers gathered and Jesus appeared to them all at the same time. If his appearances in Galilee did not happen on consecutive days then the earliest he could have been seen by his brother James was Friday, 5/5/30.

Day 28 – Saturday, 6/5/30

Jesus ascended to heaven from the Mount of Olives on his fortieth day of appearances (Acts 1:3-12), which was Thursday, 18/5/30. His disciples would have returned to Jerusalem from Galilee before that time. The only unbroken period when they could have made the five-day walk from Capernaum to the capital, without having to rest on a holy day was from Sunday, 7/5/30 to Friday, 12/5/30. Jerusalem was about ninety miles from Capernaum. If the disciples walked at about twenty miles a day, the journey would have taken five days. They could have set out on Sunday, 7/5/30 and arrived in Jerusalem on Thursday, 11/5/30 or they could have left Galilee on Monday, 8/5/30 and arrived in the capital on Friday, 12/5/30.

When the disciples were told to go to Galilee, (Matthew 28:5-10), it seems Jesus wanted them out of the capital. It implies he wanted them to stay in Galilee for the longest possible time. That would mean they would have left Capernaum on Monday, 8/5/30 at the latest. Also it would mean after his brother James saw Jesus on Friday, 5/5/30, his disciples stayed in Galilee until Monday, 8/5/30.

The day after Jesus had appeared to James, Saturday, 6/5/30 was a Sabbath. As walking long distances, which was seen as work was unlawful on the Sabbath (Leviticus 23:3), the disciples would have been unable to set out on their journey to Jerusalem that day. They would have rested in Capernaum on that holy day from sunset on Friday, 5/5/30 to sunset on Saturday, 6/5/30.

Thought

Be holy, because I am holy

Day 29

Sunday, 7/5/30

Jesus' disciples stayed in Galilee

If Jesus' disciples stayed in Galilee from 22/4/30 to 6/5/30, then the Sabbaths on 22/4/30; 29/4/30; and 6/5/30 and New Moon Festival on 24/4/30 meant there were two unbroken periods (when no holy days were held) when Jesus could have appeared there: in the four-day period, 25/4/30-28/4/30 and the six-day period, 30/4/30-5/5/30.

If his appearances in Galilee did not occur on consecutive days, his lake and mountain appearances, each lasting two days could not have occurred in the four-day period, 25/4/30-28/4/30. The earliest Jesus could have appeared by the lake was 25/4/30 to 26/4/30. His other appearances would have happened from 30/4/30 to 5/5/30. The earliest he could have appeared on a mountain in Galilee was on Sunday, 30/4/30. The disciples would have descended it the next day (Monday, 1/5/30) and put the Great Commission into practise. On Tuesday, 2/5/30, they witnessed Jesus had died for the sins of the world and had risen on the third day and they had seen him alive. By Wednesday, 3/5/30, the number of believers had grown to more than five hundred when Jesus appeared to them all at the same time. If his appearances did not happen on consecutive days, Jesus would have appeared to his brother James on Friday, 5/5/30.

Day 29 – Sunday, 7/5/30

Jesus' final appearance to his disciples was at his ascension from the Mount of Olives on Thursday, 18/5/30. To be present at that appearance they must have returned to Jerusalem from Galilee by Wednesday, 17/5/30 at the latest. The day after Jesus appeared to his brother James in Galilee, Saturday, 6/5/30 was a Sabbath. As walking long distances was seen as work, it was unlawful on the Sabbath (Leviticus 23:3), so the disciples would have been unable to set out to Jerusalem that day. They would have rested in Capernaum on the Sabbath in obedience to the Law.

The only time after James saw Jesus in which his disciples could have made an unbroken journey (when no Sabbath was held on the way) to arrive in Jerusalem to witness the Ascension was from Sunday, 7/5/30 to Friday, 12/5/30. On Resurrection Day, an angel and Jesus told them to go to Galilee (Matthew 28:5-10). It seems he wanted his disciples out of Jerusalem and in Galilee for the main period of his resurrection appearances. It would mean they would not have begun their five-day journey to Jerusalem until Monday, 8/5/30 and would have remained in Capernaum on Sunday, 7/5/30.

Thought

Behold! The Lamb of God, who takes away the sin of the world

Day 30

Monday, 8/5/30

The disciples' journey to Jerusalem

On the last of his forty days of resurrection appearances, Jesus ascended to heaven from the Mount of Olives (Acts 1:6-12). For his disciples to witness this, they must have made the ninety-mile walk from Galilee to Jerusalem before then. If they walked at twenty miles a day, it would have taken five days to get there. The only five-day period in which they could have made an unbroken journey (without a Sabbath being held on the way) to be in Jerusalem in time to see the Ascension was from, Monday, 8/5/30 to Friday, 12/5/30.

During his time of ministry, Jesus travelled from Galilee to feasts in Jerusalem. He would set out from Capernaum where his ministry was based. He visited Nazareth in his final year of ministry on the way to the Feast of Tabernacles (John 7:1-10). Luke 17:11 says on the way to Jerusalem in his final year of ministry, Jesus travelled along the Galilee and Samaria border. He passed through Samaria and stopped in a village in that area (Luke 9:51-56). The border of Galilee and Samaria was a two-day walk from Capernaum. If his disciples followed the same route, they would have set out on Monday, 8/5/30 and spent the day walking twenty miles through Galilee and would have arrived in south Galilee before sunset.

Day 30 – Monday, 8/5/30

As he bled and died for the sins of the world on the cross, Jesus placed his mother Mary into the care of John, the disciple whom he loved (John 19:25-27). John would not have left Mary and Jesus' siblings in the capital, at the mercy of the religious leaders who had conspired to have him killed and the locals who had called for his blood. John and the other disciples would have taken Jesus' family with them when they travelled to Galilee and would have brought them back to Jerusalem when they returned there. They were with the apostles in the house after the Ascension (Acts 1:12-14).

Mary's home was in Nazareth, which was in south Galilee. It would have been the perfect resting place at the end of the first day of the disciples' journey from Capernaum. Mary, in the spirit of her son would have opened up her home to them. The apostles, Mary and her children and the hundred and twenty disciples would have arrived at her home before sunset and spent the night there.

Thought

Nazareth! Can anything good come from there?

Day 31

Tuesday, 9/5/30

Journey from Nazareth to north Samaria

On the last of his forty days of resurrection appearances, Jesus ascended into heaven from the Mount of Olives (Acts 1:6-12). For his disciples to witness this, they must have made the ninety-mile walk from Galilee to Jerusalem before then. If they walked at about twenty miles a day, it would have taken five days to get there. The only five-day period in which they could have made an unbroken journey (without a Sabbath being held on the way) to be in the capital in time to see the Ascension was from 8/5/30 to 12/5/30.

Jesus often walked from Capernaum (where he based his ministry) to Jerusalem to attend feasts. He visited Nazareth on the way to the Feast of Tabernacles in his final year of ministry (John 7:1-10). He passed along the Galilee and Samaria border on his final journey to Jerusalem (Luke 17:11). As he passed through Samaria, he spent the night in a village in the border region (Luke 9:51-56). The border of Samaria was a two-day walk from Capernaum. If his disciples followed the same route to Jerusalem, they would have set out from Capernaum first thing on Monday, 8/5/30. They would have spent the day walking about twenty miles through Galilee and would have arrived in southern Galilee before sunset.

Day 31 – Tuesday, 9/5/30

Jesus' family home in Nazareth was located in southern Galilee. He visited there on his way to the Feast of Tabernacles in each of his final two years of ministry (Mark 6:1-6 and John 7:1-10). After spending the night there, he would set out the next day, walk through Galilee and crossed the border into Samaria. He would stop in a village in the border area and spend the night there (Luke 9:52-56).

As he bled and died on the cross, Jesus put his mother Mary into the care of John, his disciple (John 19:25-27). John would not have left her and the family in Jerusalem, at the mercy of the leaders who had killed Jesus. He would have taken Mary and her children to Galilee and returned to the capital with them as they were with the disciples in the house after the Ascension (Acts 1:12-14).

If the disciples left Capernaum on Monday, 8/5/30 and followed Jesus' usual route to Jerusalem, they would have spent the day walking twenty miles to Nazareth. After arriving there towards the end of the day, Mary would have opened up her home to them and they would have spent the night there. It would have been first thing the next day on Tuesday, 9/5/30 that they set out from Nazareth and walked about twenty miles through southern Galilee. The disciples and Jesus' family would have crossed the border into Samaria before sunset. They would have spent the night in a village in the border area.

Thought

Was no one found to return and give praise to God except this foreigner?

Day 32

Wednesday, 10/5/30

Journey from north Samaria to south Samaria

If Jesus' final appearance to his disciples was at his ascension from the Mount of Olives (Acts 1:6-12) on Thursday, 18/5/30, they must have returned to Jerusalem before then. The capital was about ninety miles from Capernaum. If they walked at twenty miles a day, it would have taken five days to get there. The only five-day period in which they could have made an unbroken journey (without a Sabbath being held on the way) to be there in time to see Jesus ascend into heaven to sit as God's right hand was from 8/5/30 to 12/5/30.

During his ministry when he travelled between Galilee and Jerusalem, Jesus passed through Samaria and stayed in villages there on the way (John 4:3-42). He would set out from Capernaum and pass through Galilee to Samaria, stopping in Nazareth at his family home on the way, as he did in his final year (John 7:1-10). That year, he went along the Galilee and Samaria border on the way (Luke 17:11) and spent the night in the area (Luke 9:51-56). He visited Jericho before arriving in Jerusalem (Luke 19:1-28). Jericho was a two-day walk from the Galilee border. He would stay overnight in a town in south Samaria on the way then walk to Jericho the next day. The following day, he would walk from Jericho to Jerusalem.

Day 32 – Wednesday, 10/5/30

If the disciples took Jesus' route to Jerusalem, they would have left Capernaum early on Monday, 8/5/30 and spent the day walking about twenty miles through Galilee. Nazareth is located in southern Galilee. Mary would have been with the disciples as they travelled to Jerusalem. As Jesus hung on the cross, he placed Mary into the care of John, the disciple he loved (John 19:25-27). He would have brought her and her family to Galilee when they travelled there from Jerusalem. He brought them back to Jerusalem, because they were in the house in the capital after the Ascension (Acts 1:12-14). At the end of the first day of the journey to Jerusalem, the disciples would have stopped at Mary's home in Nazareth and spent the night there.

They would have set out first thing the next day (Tuesday, 9/5/30) from Nazareth and spent that day walking about twenty miles through southern Galilee. The disciples and Mary and her family would have crossed the border into Samaria before sunset. They would have spent the night in a town or village in the border region.

The disciples would have left that town or village in the border area first thing on Wednesday, 10/5/30. They would have spent the day walking about twenty miles southwards through Samaria. They would have arrived in a town or village in south Samaria before sunset and would have spent the night there.

Thought

Look at the fields! They are ripe for harvest

Day 33

Thursday, 11/5/30

Journey from south Samaria to Jericho

Jesus' last appearance to his disciples was on the Mount of Olives when he ascended into heaven (Acts 1:6-12) on Thursday, 18/5/30. So they must have returned to Jerusalem from Galilee before then. The ninety-mile walk there would have taken five days if they walked at about twenty miles a day. The only five-day period in which they could have made an unbroken journey from Capernaum to the capital (without a holy day being held on the way) to witness the Ascension was from, Monday, 8/5/30 to Friday, 12/5/30.

When Jesus travelled from Galilee to Jerusalem and back again, he passed through Samaria on the way (John 4:3-42). He would set out from Capernaum and pass through Galilee to Samaria, stopping at his family home in Nazareth on the way (John 7:1-10). In his final year, he went along the border of Galilee and Samaria (Luke 17:11) and spent the night in a village in that area (Luke 9:51-56). Jesus visited Jericho before arriving in Jerusalem (Luke 19:1-28). Jericho was a two-day walk from the border of Galilee and Samaria. He would pass through Samaria and stay overnight in a town in south Samaria on the way then walk to Jericho the next day. On the final day of his journey, Jesus would walk from Jericho to Jerusalem.

Day 33 – Thursday, 11/5/30

If Jesus' disciples took this route when they returned to the capital, they would have set out from Capernaum early on Monday, 8/5/30. They would have spent the day walking about twenty miles and arrived in south Galilee before sunset. Jesus' family home was in Nazareth in south Galilee. His mother would have been with the disciples on this journey. As Jesus bled and died on the cross, he placed Mary into the care of John his disciple (John 19:25-27). John would not have left her and her family in Jerusalem, at the mercy of the leaders who had him killed and the residents who had called for his blood. John would have brought them to Galilee after Jesus had appeared to Thomas. John brought them back to Jerusalem, as they were in the house after the Ascension (Acts 1:12-14). After spending the day walking twenty miles from Capernaum, the disciples would have stopped at Mary's home in Nazareth and spent the night there.

They would have set out early the next day (Tuesday, 9/5/30) from Nazareth and walked about twenty miles through Galilee. They would have crossed the border into Samaria before sunset and spent the night in a village there. Next day (Wednesday, 10/5/30); they would have left that village then spent the day walking about twenty miles to south Samaria. They would have arrived in a town or village in that area before sunset and spent the night there. On Thursday, 11/5/30, they would have walked from that town in south Samaria to Jericho and arrived there before sunset. The disciples and Mary and her family would have spent the night in Jericho.

Thought

The Son of Man came to seek and save what was lost

Day 34

Friday, 12/5/30

Journey from Jericho to Jerusalem

The last time the disciples saw Jesus after he rose from the dead was at his ascension from the Mount of Olives on Thursday, 18/5/30. They must have returned there from Galilee before then to witness it. The ninety-mile walk to the capital would have taken five days if they walked at twenty miles a day. The only five-day period in which they could have made an unbroken journey (without a Sabbath being held on the way) to be in Jerusalem to witness Jesus ascend into heaven was from, Monday, 8/5/30 to Friday, 12/5/30.

When Jesus travelled to or from Jerusalem during his ministry, he set out from Capernaum and passed through Galilee to Samaria, stopping at his family home in Nazareth on the way (John 7:1-10). On previous journeys, Jesus passed through Samaria and stayed in villages there on the way (John 4:3-42). In his final year, he travelled along the Galilee and Samaria border on the way (Luke 17:11) and spent the night in a village in the border region (Luke 9:51-56). Then he visited Jericho (Luke 19:1-28), which was a two-day walk from the Galilee border. Jesus would stay the night in south Samaria on the way then walk to Jericho the next day. On the final day of his journey, he would walk from Jericho to Jerusalem.

Day 34 – Friday, 12/5/30

If the disciples followed this route to Jerusalem, they would have set out from Capernaum and spent Monday, 8/5/30 walking twenty miles to south Galilee. They would have arrived at Mary's home in Nazareth in south Galilee before sunset. She would have been with them as Jesus entrusted her to John's care (John 19:25-27). John and the disciples would have brought Mary with them to Galilee and brought her back to Jerusalem, as she was in the house after the Ascension (Acts 1:12-14). Her home in Nazareth was the perfect place to spend the night after she, her family and the disciples had spent the day walking about twenty miles from Capernaum.

On Tuesday, 9/5/30 they would have left Nazareth and walked about twenty miles through Galilee, crossing into Samaria before sunset and spending the night in a village in that area. Early, the next day, they would have left that village and spent Wednesday, 10/5/30 walking about twenty miles to south Samaria. They would have arrived in a village in that area before sunset and spent the night there. On Thursday, 11/5/30, the disciples would have walked from the village in south Samaria to Jericho and arrived there before sunset. They would have spent the night in the City of Palms.

Jesus' disciples would have left Jericho early in the morning on Friday, 12/5/30. They would have walked the fifteen miles from Jericho to the capital that day. The next day, Saturday, 13/5/30 was a Sabbath. The Eleven would have arrived in Jerusalem before the holy day began at sunset, as walking long distances, which was seen as work was unlawful on the Sabbath (Leviticus 23:3).

Thought

The last time his disciples entered Jerusalem after visiting Jericho was at Jesus' Triumphal Entry

Day 35

Saturday, 13/5/30

Sabbath celebration in Jerusalem

If the disciples' journeys to and from Galilee were unbroken, they would have timed their walks so that no holy day was celebrated as they travelled. If Jesus' appearances in Galilee took place from 22/4/30 to 5/5/30, the only unbroken period when they could have made the five-day journey to Jerusalem was from Monday, 8/5/30 to Friday, 12/5/30. They would have arrived in Jerusalem that Friday before the Sabbath began at sunset, as walking long distances was unlawful on the holy day (Leviticus 23:3).

If they arrived in Jerusalem on Friday, 12/5/30, it would have been five days before they witnessed the ascension. As Jesus appeared to them in the capital before that, it would have happened from Saturday, 13/5/30 to Wednesday, 17/5/30. Luke 24:36-49 describes this appearance in his record of resurrection events, but it reads like a continuous set of events: Jesus appeared to his disciples on Resurrection Day; he told them to stay in the city to receive the Spirit; then he led them out to the Mount of Olives and ascended into heaven. It is clear the disciples did not stay in Jerusalem from Resurrection Day until the Spirit came at Pentecost, as they went to Galilee and saw Jesus (John 20:1-23 and Matthew 28:16-20).

Day 35 – Saturday, 13/5/30

Acts 1:4-5 says on one occasion whilst the disciples were eating with Jesus, he told them to wait in Jerusalem to receive the Spirit. Then Acts 1:6 says when they met together; they asked when he would restore the kingdom of Israel. Jesus said only God knew those times then ascended to heaven before their eyes. Acts 1:4-6 shows the two appearances in Jerusalem happened on different occasions. He would have told them to stay in the city to receive the Spirit after they arrived there on Friday, 12/5/30 and before his ascension on Thursday, 18/5/30. Acts 2:1-4 says the disciples were baptised with the Holy Spirit at the Feast of Pentecost, which was celebrated ten days after Jesus ascended into heaven.

If Jesus appeared to the disciples in Jerusalem on Saturday, 13/5/30 and told them to wait in the city for the Spirit, they would have waited in the capital for fifteen days (13/5/30-28/5/30) to receive the Spirit. Fifteen days is too long to concur with Jesus' words, "*a few days*". Jesus would not have appeared to them on Saturday, 13/5/30, a Sabbath. It would have begun at sunset on Friday, 12/5/30 and ended at sunset on Saturday, 13/5/30. The disciples would have remained in Jerusalem on the Sabbath. The day of rest would have given them the opportunity to refresh themselves after their five-day walk from Capernaum in Galilee.

Thought

In the world you will have trouble. But take heart! I have overcome the world

Day 36

Sunday, 14/5/30

Jesus' disciples stayed in Jerusalem

If the disciples' journeys to and from Galilee were unbroken, they would have timed their walks so no holy day fell as they travelled. The only unbroken period when they could have made the five-day walk to the capital was from Monday, 8/5/30 to Friday, 12/5/30. They would have arrived in Jerusalem before the Sabbath began at sunset that day, as walking long distances, which was seen as work was unlawful on the Sabbath (Leviticus 23:3).

After his resurrection on Sunday, 9/4/30, Jesus appeared for forty days before he ascended into heaven (Acts 1:1-11). Forty days from Sunday, 9/4/30 is Thursday, 18/5/30. If Jesus' disciples returned from Galilee to Jerusalem on Friday, 12/5/30 then his penultimate appearance to them when he told them to stay in the city to receive the Spirit took place from Saturday, 13/5/30 to Wednesday, 17/5/30.

The Sabbath began at sunset on the day they arrived in Jerusalem (Friday, 12/5/30). Jesus' disciples would have rested that day in the capital until the Sabbath ended at sunset on Saturday, 13/5/30. The twenty-four hours of rest would have enabled them to recover from their five-day walk from Capernaum to Jerusalem.

Day 36 – Sunday, 14/5/30

Whilst the disciples were in Jerusalem after returning from Galilee, Jesus appeared to them on one occasion whilst they were eating in the house. He told them not to leave Jerusalem but to wait in the city until they received the gift his Father had promised: the baptism of the Holy Spirit (Acts 1:4-5). He could not have said this at his appearances to them on Resurrection Day (9/4/30) or a week later (16/4/30) as the disciples went to Galilee after that appearance.

If Jesus' appearance occurred after they returned to Jerusalem and before his ascension, it happened in the period, Saturday, 13/5/30 to Wednesday, 17/5/30. Jesus' words to his disciples were fulfilled when they were baptised in the Holy Spirit at the Feast of Pentecost. This feast was held fifty days after the day Jesus rose from the dead. If he ascended into heaven on the fortieth day of his resurrection appearances then they would have been filled with the Holy Spirit on Sunday, 28/5/30 – ten days after the Ascension.

When he told his disciples to stay in the city, to receive the gift God had promised, he said they would be baptised with the Spirit in a few days. If he said this on the day after they arrived (Saturday, 13/5/30), it would have been fifteen days before the Ascension. If he told them to wait there for the Holy Spirit on Sunday, 14/5/30, that would have been two weeks before they were filled with the Holy Spirit at Pentecost. If Jesus appeared to them on either of those days, it was fourteen or fifteen days before the Feast of Pentecost. That length of time does not agree with Jesus' words, 'in a few days.' So they would have stayed in Jerusalem on Sunday, 14/5/30.

Thought

You will receive power when the Holy Spirit comes on you

Day 37

Monday, 15/5/30

Jesus' disciples stayed in Jerusalem

If the disciples left Jerusalem the day after Jesus had appeared to Thomas (17/4/30), it would have taken five days to walk to Galilee if they walked at twenty miles a day. They would have arrived there on Friday, 21/4/30. If Jesus' final appearance in Galilee (to James) was on Friday, 5/5/30, the latest they could have made a five-day walk to Jerusalem without a Sabbath being held on the way, was from Monday, 8/5/30 to Friday, 12/5/30. They would have arrived in Jerusalem before the Sabbath began at sunset that day, as walking long distances was unlawful on Sabbaths (Leviticus 23:3).

After his resurrection on Sunday, 9/4/30, Jesus appeared for forty days before his ascension (Acts 1:1-3) on Thursday, 18/5/30. If his disciples arrived in Jerusalem on Friday, 12/5/30, He would have told them to wait in the city to receive the Spirit from Saturday, 13/5/30 to Wednesday, 17/5/30. After they arrived back in Jerusalem, they would have rested on the Sabbath from sunset on Friday, 12/5/30 until sunset on Saturday, 13/5/30. The twenty-four hour period of rest would have enabled Jesus' disciples to recoup from their five-day walk from Capernaum in Galilee to Jerusalem.

Day 37 – Monday, 15/5/30

After the disciples returned to Jerusalem and before his ascension, Jesus appeared to them whilst they were eating. He told them not to leave the city, but to wait there until they received the gift his Father had promised; the baptism of the Holy Spirit (Acts 1:4-5). His penultimate appearance to his disciples would have occurred from Saturday, 13/5/30 to Wednesday, 17/5/30. They were filled with the Holy Spirit at the Feast of Pentecost, which was celebrated ten days after Jesus ascended into heaven – that is Sunday, 28/5/30.

When Jesus appeared to his disciples, he told them they would be baptised by the Spirit, *'in a few days'*. This helps pinpoint when this appearance occurred after they arrived in Jerusalem. Their first weekend there after they returned from Galilee (Saturday, 13/5/30 to Sunday, 14/5/30) was fourteen to fifteen days before Pentecost. Monday, 15/5/30 would have been thirteen days before they were filled with the Holy Spirit. Thirteen to fifteen days is too long a timeframe to concur with Jesus' statement of, 'in a few days'. If Jesus did not appear to his disciples on Monday, 15/5/30, then they would have remained in Jerusalem that day.

Thought

No one can see the kingdom of God unless he is born again

Day 38

Tuesday, 16/5/30

Jesus' disciples stayed in Jerusalem

If Jesus' disciples' journeys to and from Galilee were unbroken, they would have timed their walks so that no Sabbath or holy day was held as they travelled. The latest unbroken period they could have returned to Jerusalem before the Ascension was from 8/5/30 to 12/5/30. They would have arrived in the capital before the Sabbath began at sunset on Friday, 12/5/30 – five days before Jesus' final appearance at his ascension into heaven on Thursday, 18/5/30.

So Jesus' penultimate appearance to the disciples occurred from Saturday, 13/5/30 to Wednesday, 17/5/30. Jesus said they would be baptised in the Spirit in a few days. It happened at Pentecost. The length of time each day from 13/5/30 to 17/5/30 is from Pentecost (28/5/30) will reveal which date is the fewest days from that feast:

How long the disciples waited in Jerusalem

13/5/30 = 15 days to the Feast of Pentecost
14/5/30 = 14 days to the Feast of Pentecost
15/5/30 = 13 days to the Feast of Pentecost
16/5/30 = 12 days to the Feast of Pentecost
17/5/30 = 11 days to the Feast of Pentecost

Day 38 – Tuesday, 16/5/30

If Jesus told his disciples to stay in Jerusalem on any of the days from Saturday, 13/5/30 to Wednesday, 17/5/30, his appearance to them would have happened from eleven to fifteen days before they were baptised with the Holy Spirit at Pentecost (Sunday, 28/5/30).

Nowadays, we regard 'a few days' as around three days. However, it is clear that was not the case in Jesus' time. Despite this, twelve, thirteen, fourteen or fifteen days could not be described as, 'a few days'. It means Jesus could not have told his disciples to wait in the city for the Holy Spirit on Saturday, 13/5/30; Sunday, 14/5/30; Monday, 15/5/30; or Tuesday, 16/5/30. So, Tuesday, 16/5/30 would have been one of the days Jesus' disciples stayed in Jerusalem.

Thought

When he the Spirit of Truth comes, he will guide you into all truth

Day 39

Wednesday, 17/5/30

Risen Jesus appeared to the Eleven

After his death, Jesus rose to life on the third day, Sunday, 9/4/30. He appeared to his disciples for forty days and his final appearance was at his ascension from the Mount of Olives (Acts 1:1-12). Forty days from Sunday, 9/4/30 is Thursday, 18/5/30. If the disciples left the capital on Monday, 17/4/30 after Thomas saw Jesus (John 20:26-29), they would have arrived in Galilee five days later on Friday, 21/4/30. He appeared four times in Galilee. His final appearance there was to James on Friday, 5/5/30. The latest they could have made an unbroken return journey to Jerusalem (when no Sabbath was celebrated on the way) to witness Jesus' ascension into heaven would have been from Monday, 8/5/30 to Friday, 12/5/30.

If this was the timeframe for his disciples' movements during his forty days of appearances, they would have arrived in Jerusalem before the Sabbath began at sunset on Friday, 12/5/30. If Jesus ascended into heaven on Thursday, 18/5/30, they spent five days (13/5/30 to 17/5/30) in the capital before his final appearance. The Ascension was not Jesus' only appearance to his disciples after they returned to Jerusalem from Galilee, so his penultimate resurrection appearance to them would have occurred in that five-day period.

Day 39 – Wednesday, 17/5/30

His penultimate appearance occurred this way: '*On one occasion, while Jesus was eating with them, he gave this command, "Do not leave Jerusalem, but wait for the gift my Father promised, which you have heard me speak about. For John baptised with water, but in a few days you will be baptised with the Holy Spirit*" (Acts 1:4-5).

Jesus told them this from Saturday, 13/5/30 to Wednesday, 17/5/30. Acts 1:6-7 says the Spirit came at Pentecost (Sunday, 28/5/30), ten days after the Ascension. If each date from 13/5/30 to 17/5/30 is deducted from 28/5/30, it shows how long they waited in the city:

How long the disciples waited

13/5/30 = 15 days to the Feast of Pentecost
14/5/30 = 14 days to the Feast of Pentecost
15/5/30 = 13 days to the Feast of Pentecost
16/5/30 = 12 days to the Feast of Pentecost
17/5/30 = 11 days to the Feast of Pentecost

If Jesus' penultimate appearance occurred from 13/5/30 to 17/5/30, the disciples waited eleven to fifteen days to receive the Spirit at Pentecost on 28/5/30. Today, 'a few days' is regarded as three, but not in Jesus' time. Yet twelve, thirteen, fourteen or fifteen days could not be described as, 'a few days'. It means Jesus could not have told his disciples to wait in Jerusalem from Saturday, 13/5/30 to Tuesday, 16/5/30. Wednesday, 17/5/30 was eleven days before the Feast of Pentecost (the shortest time span for the above dates), so it is the most likely day Jesus told the disciples to wait in Jerusalem.

Thought

Trust in the Lord with all your heart and lean not on your own understanding

Day 40

Thursday, 18/5/30

Risen Jesus ascended into heaven

After Jesus rose from the dead on the third day after his crucifixion (Sunday, 9/5/30), he was seen by his disciples over a period of forty days (Acts 1:1-3). Four appearances were in Galilee, which Jesus' disciples visited from 17/4/30 to 12/5/30. He appeared to them twice after they returned to Jerusalem. At Jesus' final appearance, he met with his disciples and led them out to the Mount of Olives.

'They asked him, "Lord, are you at this time going to restore the kingdom of Israel?" He said to them, "It is not for you to know the times or dates the Father has set by his own authority. But you will receive power when the Holy Spirit comes on you, and you will be my witnesses in Jerusalem, and in all Judea and Samaria, and to the ends of the earth." After he said this he was taken up before their very eyes, and a cloud hid him from their sight. They were looking intently up into the sky as he was going, when suddenly two men dressed in white stood beside them. "Men of Galilee," they said, "why do you stand here looking into the sky? This same Jesus, who has been taken from you into heaven, will come back in the same way you have seen him go into heaven"' (Acts 1:6-11).

Day 40 – Thursday, 18/5/30

If Jesus appeared to his disciples for forty days after his resurrection (Acts 1:1-3), his final appearance to them at his ascension occurred on the fortieth day of his appearances. Jesus rose from the dead on the third day after he died on the cross of Calvary for the sins of the world. The day he died was the Passover (John 18:28), which was held on a Friday that year (John 19:31). In that era, the Passover was held on a Friday twice: on April 7th 30AD and April 5th 33AD.

It was shown in 'the Jesus Diary[1]', Part One of The Chronology of Jesus' Life series that he died on Friday the Seventh of April in 30AD. Luke 24:21 says he rose to life on the third day. So, Resurrection Day would have occurred on Sunday, 9/4/30. Forty days from Sunday, 9/4/30 is Thursday, 18/5/30. Jesus Christ, the Son of God, who is God, would have ascended to heaven to sit at the right hand of God, his heavenly Father on Thursday, 18/5/30.

It seems Jesus' final two appearances to his disciples happened on the last two days of his forty days of appearances. In his penultimate appearance to them on Wednesday, 17/5/30, he told them to stay in the city as in a few days they would be baptised with the Holy Spirit (Acts 1:4-5). The same Spirit, life, authority and power that had been in Jesus would be in all of his disciples. And the next day, as they watched him ascend into heaven they learned that their Lord and Saviour, the King of kings and Lord of lords would return in the same way they had seen him go – Hallelujah!

Thought

Come, Lord Jesus, come!

Summary of Jesus' appearances

Resurrection Day – Sunday, 9/4/30

Jesus rose from the dead
Jesus appeared to the women from Galilee[1*]
Jesus appeared to Mary Magdalene[2*]
Jesus appeared to Peter[3]
Jesus appeared to two disciples at Emmaus[4]
Jesus appeared to the Apostles[5]

Monday, 10/4/30 to Friday, 14/4/30

Jesus' disciples stayed in Jerusalem

Saturday, 15/4/30

Sabbath celebration in Jerusalem

Sunday, 16/4/30

Jesus appeared to Thomas[6]

Monday, 17/4/30 to Friday, 21/4/30

Jesus' disciples travelled to Galilee

Saturday, 22/4/30

Sabbath celebration in Galilee

Sunday, 23/4/30

Jesus' disciples stayed in Galilee

Monday, 24/4/30

New Moon celebration in Galilee

Tuesday, 25/4/30 to Wednesday, 26/4/30

Peter fished all night on the Sea of Galilee
Jesus appeared by the Sea of Galilee[7]

Thursday, 27/4/30 to Friday, 28/4/30

Jesus' disciples stayed in Galilee

Saturday, 29/4/30

Sabbath celebration in Galilee

Sunday, 30/4/30 to Friday, 5/5/30

Jesus appeared on a mountain in Galilee[8*]
Jesus' disciples stayed in Galilee
Jesus appeared to over five hundred men in Galilee[9*]
Jesus appeared to James in Galilee[10]

Saturday, 6/5/30

Sabbath celebration in Galilee

Sunday, 7/5/30

Jesus' disciples stayed in Galilee

Monday, 8/5/30 to Friday, 12/5/30

Jesus' disciples travelled to Jerusalem

Saturday, 13/5/30

Sabbath celebration in Jerusalem

Sunday, 14/5/30 to Tuesday, 16/5/30

Jesus' disciples stayed in Jerusalem

Wednesday, 17/5/30

Jesus told the Eleven to wait in the Jerusalem for the Spirit[11]

Thursday, 18/5/30

Jesus ascended into heaven[12]

Jesus' twelve appearances

According to Scripture, after rising from the dead, Jesus appeared twelve times in forty days: eight times in Jerusalem (on four separate days); and four times in Galilee (on four separate days):

Sunday, 9/4/30

1. Jesus appeared to the women at the tomb in Jerusalem
2. Jesus appeared to Mary at the tomb in Jerusalem
3. Jesus appeared to Peter in Jerusalem
4. Jesus appeared to two disciples at Emmaus
5. Jesus appeared to the Apostles in the house in Jerusalem

Sunday, 16/4/30 in Jerusalem

6. Jesus appeared to Thomas in the house in Jerusalem

Wednesday, 26/4/30

7. Jesus appeared to his disciples by the Sea of Galilee

Sunday, 30/4/30

8. Jesus appeared to the disciples on a Galilean mountain

Wednesday, 3/5/30

9. Jesus appeared to over five hundred brothers in Galilee

Friday, 5/5/30

10. Jesus appeared to his brother James in Galilee

Wednesday, 17/5/30

11. Jesus told the Eleven to wait in Jerusalem for the Holy Spirit

Thursday, 18/5/30

12. The disciples saw Jesus' ascension from the Mount of Olives

Witnesses to the Resurrection

The women from Galilee

At dawn, on Resurrection Day, Mary Magdalene, Salome, James' mother Mary and others went to the tomb (Matthew 28:1; Mark 16:1; and Luke 24:1-10). For there to be other women, there must have been at least two others. So, as well as the three who were named at least five women visited the tomb and were told by the angels to tell the disciples Jesus had risen. As they went to tell the disciples, Jesus appeared to them (Matthew 28:8-10).

Mary Magdalene

Mark 16:9-11 and John 20:10-18 say Jesus' first appearance was to Mary Magdalene. They record it after Peter visited the empty tomb, after the women had returned to the house and reported all they had seen. If we believe what is written in the Bible, the appearance to Mary after Peter had visited the tomb cannot be the same as the appearance to the women, which occurred before he visited the tomb. Mary must have rushed to the house after seeing the empty tomb and reported it to the disciples. The other women stayed at the tomb, were spoken to by angels and saw risen Jesus as they returned to the house. After speaking to the disciples, Peter, John and Mary would have gone to the tomb. Then it was after Peter and John had returned home that Jesus appeared to Mary Magdalene.

Peter

The first man Jesus appeared to on Resurrection Day was Peter, who had denied him three times. At this meeting, Peter's conscience was restored, but his ministry was restored later in Galilee. The Lord chose not to record the events of this meeting in the Bible. It took place after Jesus had appeared to Mary and before he was seen at Emmaus, as the two disciples who saw him there, told the Apostles Jesus had appeared to Peter (Luke 24:34). Also this appearance to Peter is recorded in 1 Corinthians 15:5.

Two disciples at Emmaus

Luke 24:13-32 says Jesus appeared to two disciples on the road to Emmaus, but they did not recognise him. Then he discussed with them all the Scriptures concerning himself. From his perspective, it was more important for the two disciples to see and recognise him from the Scriptures than it was for them to see and recognise him in person. They arrived in Emmaus and ate some food. As Jesus broke bread, their eyes were opened and they saw it was him. All Scripture pointed to Jesus' death and resurrection and breaking bread is the commemoration of his loving sacrifice.

Ten apostles and the hundred and twenty

At Jesus' appearance in the house on Resurrection Day, Thomas was absent (John 20:24). Others were there (Luke 24:9 and Luke 24:33). The others with the Eleven in the house that day were the one hundred and twenty disciples who were with them in that house, after Jesus ascended into heaven (Acts 1:15).

Eleven apostles and the hundred and twenty

The next time Jesus appeared to his apostles was a week later in the house in Jerusalem and Thomas was present (John 20:26-29). Now, in 1 Corinthians 15:3-5, Paul says twelve apostles were there. He included Matthias, who was at each appearance and later replaced Judas as one of the twelve apostles (Acts 1:15-26). The hundred and twenty disciples would have been there as well, as they were on Resurrection Day and after the Ascension (Acts 1:15).

Peter and six disciples

After Jesus appeared to Thomas, his disciples went to Galilee (Matthew 28:16-20 and John 21:1-23). Whilst they were there, Peter and six others fished all night on the lake, but they caught nothing. At dawn the next day, Jesus appeared to them by the lake and supplied them with a miraculous catch of fish. Then Jesus fed his disciples, before restoring Peter to his ministry (John 21:1-23).

Eleven apostles and the hundred and twenty

When Jesus appeared on a Galilean mountain some disciples doubted (Matthew 28:16-17). It would have been some of the hundred and twenty who doubted, not the Apostles, as most of them had seen Jesus four times by then. It seems the hundred and twenty received the Great Commission and returned to Jerusalem with the Eleven. They were with them after the Ascension and when the Holy Spirit came at Pentecost (Acts 1:15-2:4). So along with the apostles they were empowered to carry out Jesus' Great Commission they had all received on the Galilean mountain.

More than five hundred brothers

1 Corinthians 15:6 says over five hundred brothers saw Jesus at the same time. It is not the same appearance as the mountain one as the hundred and twenty disciples were with the Eleven that time and received the Great Commission. It was they who returned to Jerusalem, saw the Ascension and received the Holy Spirit with the Eleven to carry out the Great Commission. They would have been there when Jesus appeared to over five hundred brothers.

James

After Jesus appeared to more than five hundred brothers at the same time, he appeared to his brother James (1 Corinthians 15:7).

Eleven apostles and the hundred and twenty

After returning from Galilee, Jesus told his disciples to wait in Jerusalem for the Holy Spirit. The hundred and twenty would have been there as they were after the Ascension (Acts 1:4-15).

Eleven apostles and the hundred and twenty

Jesus led his disciples out to the Mount of Olives. The eleven apostles watched him ascend into heaven. The one hundred and twenty would have been there as well, as they were in the house in Jerusalem with them after Jesus' ascension (Acts 1:12-15).

Witnesses to the Resurrection

Mark 16:1 and Luke 24:1-10 say Mary Magdalene; Salome, Mary the mother of James and other women visited Jesus' tomb. Then Mathew 28:8-10 says Jesus appeared to them. To be other women, there must have been at least two, making five in all (**5+ witnesses**). Mark 16:9-11 and John 20:10-18 say Jesus first appeared to Mary Magdalene (**1 witness**). Luke 24:34 and 1 Corinthians 15:5 say he appeared to Peter (**1 witness**). Luke 24:13-32 says after that he appeared to two disciples on the road to Emmaus (**2 witnesses**) before appearing to his disciples in the house. Ten apostles were there with Thomas absent (John 20:24), but Luke 24:9 says others were there – the hundred and twenty who were in the house after the Ascension (Acts 1:15), making a total of one hundred and thirty believers (**130 witnesses**). Jesus appeared to them a week later in the house and Thomas was present (John 20:26-29). The hundred and twenty other believers would have been there, as they were on Resurrection Day and after the Ascension (**131 witnesses**).

In Galilee, Peter and six others saw him by the lake (**7 witnesses**) then the hundred and twenty disciples and the Eleven saw him on a mountain in Galilee (**131 witnesses**). Next he appeared to over five hundred brothers (1 Corinthians 15:6-7) including the Eleven and the hundred and twenty (**500+ witnesses**) and then he appeared to James (**1 witness**). After the Eleven returned to Jerusalem, Jesus told his disciples to wait there for the Spirit. If the hundred and twenty believers were with the apostles in the house when the Spirit came at Pentecost, it would have been in obedience to Jesus' order to stay in the city until they received the Spirit (**131 witnesses**). Then at the Mount of Olives, the Eleven watched him ascend into heaven and the hundred and twenty believers were there as well just as they were in the house after the Ascension (**131 witnesses**). The number of people who saw Jesus over his forty days of appearances is one thousand, two hundred and seventy-one as shown below:
1271 = Witnesses to the Resurrection

Witnesses to the Resurrection

Place	No.	The witnesses
The tomb	..5+	Mary, James' mother, Joanna, Salome and some other women
The tomb	..1	Mary Magdalene
Jerusalem	1	**Peter**
Emmaus	2	Two disciples
Jerusalem	130	**Peter**, James, John, Andrew, Philip, Jude, Nathaniel, Matthew, James, Simon and the hundred and twenty believers
Jerusalem	131	**Peter**, James, John, Andrew, Philip, Thomas, Jude, Nathaniel, Matthew, James, Simon and the hundred and twenty believers
The lake	7	**Peter**, James, John, Nathaniel, Thomas and two other disciples
Mountain	131	**Peter**, James, John, Andrew, Philip, Thomas, Jude, Nathaniel, Matthew, James, Simon and the hundred and twenty believers
Galilee	500+	**Peter**, James, John, Andrew, Philip, Thomas, Jude, Nathaniel, Matthew, James, Simon and the hundred and twenty believers
Galilee	1	James, Jesus' brother
Jerusalem	131	**Peter**, James, John, Andrew, Philip, Thomas, Jude, Nathaniel, Matthew, James, Simon and the hundred and twenty believers
Ascension	131	**Peter**, James, John, Andrew, Philip, Thomas, Jude, Nathaniel, Matthew, James, Simon and the hundred and twenty believers
Total	**1171+**	**Witnesses to the Resurrection**

Risen Jesus appeared to Peter eight times

Jesus appeared to his disciples twelve times over forty days, be it as individuals or in groups. One time he appeared to over five hundred believers at the same time. Many saw him several times. The person he appeared to most was Peter, who saw Jesus eight times. Now let's look at the times when his disciples did not see Jesus to see what they reveal about him, his disciples and what it means to us.

Jesus' absences

Days when Jesus appeared to his disciples

Jesus was seen by his disciples on eight separate days:

Days when Jesus appeared to his disciples

09/04/30 = Jesus appeared five times on Resurrection Day
16/04/30 = Thomas saw Jesus in the house in Jerusalem
26/04/30 = Jesus appeared to Peter by the Sea of Galilee
30/04/30 = The Eleven saw Jesus on a Galilean mountain
03/05/30 = More than five hundred brothers saw Jesus
05/05/30 = Jesus appeared to his brother James in Galilee
17/05/30 = Jesus told his disciples to wait in Jerusalem
18/05/30 = Jesus' disciples witnessed his ascension

Days when Jesus did not appear to his disciples

If Jesus appeared to his disciples on eight separate days, there were thirty-two of his forty days of resurrection appearances when the disciples did not see Jesus. If he appeared on 9/4/30; 16/4/30; 26/4/30; 30/4/30; 3/5/30; 5/5/30; 17/5/30; and 18/5/30 then Jesus would not have appeared to his disciples in the following periods:

Days when Jesus did not appear to his disciples

10/4/30 to 15/4/30 = 6 days
17/4/30 to 25/4/30 = 9 days
27/4/30 to 29/4/30 = 3 days
01/5/30 to 02/5/30 = 2 days
04/5/30   = 1 day
06/5/30 to 16/5/30 = 11 days

Over the forty days of resurrection appearances, the disciples did not see Jesus for a maximum of eleven days (Saturday, 6/5/30 to Tuesday, 16/5/30) and a minimum of one day (Thursday, 4/5/30).

Jesus' absences

Time between 1st and 2nd days of appearances

After rising from the dead on Sunday, 9/4/30, Jesus appeared five times to his disciples that day. His next appearance, to Thomas was a week later, Sunday, 16/4/30. On the six days between his first two appearances (Monday, 10/4/30 to Saturday, 15/4/30), the final six days of the Feast of Unleavened Bread were celebrated. It was one of three feasts God commanded all Jews to attend each year in Jerusalem (Deuteronomy 16:16). In obedience to God's word, the disciples would have remained in Jerusalem for that time.

When he appeared to them on Resurrection Day (Sunday, 9/4/30), his disciples were locked in the house for fear of the Jews (John 20:19). When he appeared in the house a week later (Sunday, 16/4/30), they were still locked in the house (John 20:26). It seems they spent the time between the two appearances (10/4/30-15/4/30) living in fear behind the bolted doors of the house in Jerusalem.

The first thing Jesus did at each appearance was to give them his peace. Jesus' peace was the best antidote for their fear and it is the best antidote for our fear as well. Jesus' peace transcends all understanding. To experience his peace it needs to be received. It seems his disciples did not receive it at his first appearance and spent a further week in a fearful state locked in the house.

From this we learn fear paralyses us and stops us moving out in life. It imprisons us in a place we do not want to be. It prevents us from being in the place Jesus wants us to be and being the person he has called us to be. It was only after he gave his disciples his peace at his second appearance in the house that they left for Galilee the next day. When we have Jesus' peace, nothing that happens in our world or any circumstances that arise in our lives will disturb that peace.

10/4/30-15/4/30 = Time between 1st and 2nd days of appearances

Time between 2nd and 3rd days of appearances

At Jesus' second appearance to his disciples on Sunday, 16/4/30, Thomas' angst of having to wait a week longer to see Jesus alive was replaced by his joy of acknowledging he was God. His waiting on God's timing achieved a greater purpose than just seeing Jesus had risen. It revealed he was both the Son of God and was God. In fact Thomas should be remembered for this and not his doubting, as it moved him and all the disciples forward in their faith.

It is crucial to wait on God's timing and not miss His bigger purpose in our lives. Jesus did it when he raised Lazarus from the dead. If he had not waited two days after hearing Lazarus was ill (John 11:6), it would have been another great healing. Waiting on God's timing not only raised Lazarus to life, but it revealed Jesus as the Resurrection and the Life. So at Jesus' second appearance to his apostles, the dynamic of his deity came into all their belief systems through Thomas' revelation. When we wait on God our heavenly Father and His timing, we will see more of the nature and character of Jesus and of God in the circumstances in which He places us.

On Resurrection Day, the angel at the empty tomb and Jesus told the women to tell his disciples to go to Galilee (Matthew 28:5-10). From that day to the day Thomas saw Jesus (9/4/30-16/4/30), the disciples stayed in Jerusalem. Yet, after his deity was revealed, the first thing they did was to go to Galilee. Only after Thomas caught up with the others in seeing his Lord and moved them forward by his revelation of Jesus' deity did they finally exit Jerusalem. It is only when we see Jesus is the Son of God, who is God, who died for our sins on the cross of Calvary, was buried and rose again on the third day that we are set free. We are set free from sin, disease and death and from all that binds us in life. We exit the old way of life and enter the new way of life. We are no longer bound by fear or anything in life. We are free to go where Jesus wants us to go and to be all he wants us to be. What a wonderful, loving Saviour we have in Jesus.

The disciples spent five days (Monday, 17/4/30 to Friday, 21/4/30) walking from Jerusalem to Galilee. They would have arrived there before the Sabbath began at sunset that Friday. The day of rest would have ended at sunset on Saturday, 22/4/30. As the disciples spent the night fishing before Jesus appeared to them, this appearance could not have begun on 22/4/30, as fishing was unlawful on Sabbaths. Monday, 24/4/30 was a New Moon Festival and was a day of rest. His lake appearance could not have occurred then either, as the disciples fished on both days (John 21:1-14).

Because of the Sabbath and the New Moon Festival, the two days of rest meant Jesus' appearance by the lake could not have taken place from 22/4/30 to 24/4/30. The three days of rest would have helped the disciples recover from their five-day walk to Galilee from Jerusalem and from the emotional turmoil of all they had witnessed regarding Jesus' crucifixion and resurrection. This is the beauty of Jesus. He knows everything about us and what is best for us. He knows all we have been through and are going through. Jesus is our restorer and knows when we need rest and he makes it possible.

The earliest he could have appeared by the lake after his disciples arrived in Galilee was Wednesday, 26/4/30 after Peter had spent the previous night, Tuesday, 25/4/30, fishing. At his next appearance in Galilee, Matthew 27:16 says they went to the mountain where he had told them to go. It seems he did not instruct Peter and the others to go fishing. The fact they caught nothing suggests they went out fishing under their own authority and not under Jesus' authority.

It is a lesson for us. If we do things without Jesus and do not wait on his timing, the results will be fruitless. Next day, Jesus appeared on the shore of the Sea of Galilee and provided them with a miraculous catch of fish. When they came ashore, they found Jesus cooking fish on a fire. He had what they had spent the whole night working for (John 21:1-14). Jesus always has everything we are looking for.
17/4/30-25/4/30 = Time between 2nd and 3rd days of appearances

Time between 3rd and 4th days of appearances

If Jesus' appearances in Galilee did not happen on consecutive days and he appeared by the lake on Wednesday, 26/4/30 then he could not have appeared to his disciples on a Galilean mountain on Thursday, 27/4/30. This appearance could not have happened on Friday, 28/4/30, as the next day was a Sabbath, Saturday, 29/4/30. The disciples would not have been able to descend the mountain that day (or climb it), as it was seen as work, which was unlawful on the Sabbath (Leviticus 23:3). The earliest that Jesus could have appeared on the mountain in Galilee was Sunday, 30/4/30.

There were three days (Thursday, 27/4/30 to Saturday, 29/4/30) between the appearances by the lake and on a Galilean mountain. The lake appearance marked a huge change in the disciples' belief system. The first time they saw Jesus alive on Resurrection Day after his crucifixion, they did not believe (Luke 24:36-41). When he appeared to them by the lake, they did not doubt (John 21:12).

It is the same for us as well. The more we see that Jesus is the Son of God who is God, who died on the cross of Calvary for the sins of the world, was buried and rose again on the third day, the greater our faith in him will be. We can only see these things by the revelation of the Holy Spirit in us. We see by reading, hearing and knowing the Word of God. The more we familiarise ourselves with Scripture, the more we will see that God, in His great love for us sent His beloved Son to die for our sins. We see He sent the most precious person in His life – the one He loves the most – the one He has always loved and will always love to die in excruciating pain on the cross to atone for all of our sins. All these truths are found in His word. The more we listen to sermons that point to Jesus Christ, the Son of God, who is God and his loving, selfless sacrifice on the cross, the more real he becomes. Like the disciples after the resurrection, we will no longer doubt Jesus. We will know that Jesus is Lord – Lord of all.

27/4/30-29/4/30 = Time between 3rd and 4th days of appearances

Time between 4th and 5th days of appearances

If Jesus appeared on a Galilean mountain on Sunday, 30/4/30 and his disciples descended it on Monday, 1/5/30 and his appearances did not happen on consecutive days; he could not have been seen by over five hundred brothers on Tuesday, 2/5/30. It seems after descending the mountain; his disciples put the Great Commission into practise and witnessed to Jesus' death and resurrection with others. When a crowd of over five hundred believers had gathered, Jesus appeared to them all. The earliest it could have happened was Wednesday, 3/5/30, two days after his mountain appearance.

The disciples were obedient to Jesus' words – they went to the mountain where he had told them to go (Matthew 28:16). When they came down the mountain, they put his Great Commission into practise. They did it so effectively, that the number of believers that gathered around them grew to more than five hundred. From this we see that obedience is a key part of our relationship with Jesus. When we obey Jesus, like the disciples we will always be in the right place at the right time. It will be the place Jesus wants us to be. When we obey and do what he has asked us to do, the results will be abundant.
1/5/30-2/5/30 = Time between 4th and 5th days of appearances

Time between 5th and 6th days of appearances

If Jesus did not appear to over five hundred brothers and to James on consecutive days, he could not have appeared to his brother on Thursday, 4/5/30. The earliest James could have seen Jesus was Friday, 5/5/30. In his final year of ministry, James teased him about going to the Feast of Tabernacles (John 7:1-9). After his ascension – James prayed with the apostles in the house (Acts 1:14). Maybe when he saw Jesus alive again, James believed he was God. The Lord appeared individually to James and Peter, the leaders of his Church to reveal his deity to them and increase their faith to prepare them for ministry. It is something that Jesus does for us today as well.
4/5/30 = Time between 5th and 6th days of appearances

Time between 6th and 7th days of appearances

After his resurrection, Jesus wanted his disciples in Galilee, away from Jerusalem (Matthew 28:5-10). If they stayed there for as long as possible before returning to the capital, the only time (after Jesus appeared to James), they could have made a five-day unbroken journey from Galilee, without resting on a Sabbath on the way was from Monday, 8/5/30 to Friday, 12/5/30. They would have arrived in Jerusalem before the Sabbath began at sunset that Friday then rested until the Sabbath ended at sunset on Saturday, 13/5/30.

Jesus would have told his disciples to stay in Jerusalem to receive the Spirit (Acts 1:3-4) from the day they arrived there (12/5/30) to the day before his ascension (17/5/30). He said the Spirit would come in a few days. He came at Pentecost (Sunday, 28/5/30). Today, a few days is three days, but not in Jesus' day. 12/5/30 was sixteen days before Pentecost. 17/5/30 was eleven days before. Twelve to sixteen days is too long a period to be, 'a few days.' If it was the shortest timeframe of eleven days Jesus was referring to, he would have told them to stay in the city on Wednesday, 17/5/30. They obeyed his words. Last time they were in Jerusalem, they stayed in the house out of fear. Over forty days of appearances, they moved from fearful obedience to trusting obedience. Jesus learned trusting obedience by what he suffered (Hebrews 5:8). We too can learn to obey God and trust God in Jesus Christ who loves us.

6/5/30-16/5/30 = Time between 6th and 7th days of appearances

Time between 7th and 8th days of appearances

If he told his disciples to wait for the Spirit on Wednesday, 17/5/30, it was the next day Thursday, 18/5/30 when he ascended into heaven. When his disciples asked when his kingdom would come, Jesus said only his Father knew the time. Then Jesus drew their attention back to his Great Commission to make disciples of all nations. Like his disciples that day, Jesus wants us to focus on the task he has given us and not be distracted by other things.

Why risen Jesus appeared for forty days

The disciples were with Jesus for three and a half years before he died on the cross and was buried. After his resurrection, most of them saw Jesus six times in forty days. He could have stayed with them for the whole time, but he did not. There was a purpose in the timing of his appearances. There were eleven days between some of them and just one day between others. Jesus was preparing his disciples for life without him. If he had left them after they had seen him on Resurrection Day, such a withdrawal may have shattered their faith. They were entering a time when he was not going to be with them visibly, but experientially through the Holy Spirit. In the time after they received the Spirit at Pentecost, they always acted as if Jesus was with them. He was not with them physically. Jesus was in heaven, but the Holy Spirit made his presence universal.

Over Jesus' forty days of resurrection appearances, he showed his disciples he was the Christ, the Son of God, who was God. He showed he fulfilled all the Scriptures about him. They had to fully understand this, so they could witness this truth to others. It began on the Emmaus road when he went through all the Scriptures concerning himself. It was after he explained the Scriptures and broke bread that the pair saw it was Jesus. It was more important for them to recognise him from the Scriptures than it was for them to see him physically. And today, no one is at a disadvantage to them as God's word is available to all and His Son is revealed on every page.

It took forty days for Jesus' disciples to know he was the fulfilment of all of the Scriptures. After his ascension, they had the Law, the Prophets, and Psalms to confirm their testimony Jesus was the Christ and they had seen him die on the cross and rise on the third day. As Christians we need to know and believe and live out the fact Jesus is God's Son and he is God and is the fulfilment of all that is written about him in the Bible. Then his death and resurrection will be as real to us as they were to his disciples who witnessed them.

Locations of Jesus' appearances

Jesus appeared eight times to his disciples in Jerusalem: twice at the empty tomb; three times in the house; once on the Mount of Olives; once in an unknown location and at Emmaus. He was seen four times in Galilee: by the lake; on a mountain and twice in unknown locations. Let's see what these locations reveal.

The empty tomb

Jesus' first appearances were at the empty tomb. It is where the resurrection story begins. The women and the disciples' journey began there and it is where our journey begins. Once we have seen Jesus died for our sins on the cross, the next stop of our salvation story is the empty grave. There we see and believe he died for our sins and rose victoriously over them and death.

The road to Emmaus

The two disciples on the Emmaus road told Jesus all the action was happening in Jerusalem (Luke 24:18-24). He showed his love to them even when they were heading in the wrong direction. He came to them, listened to them, revealed himself to them and brought them to where he wanted them to be. He does the same today and reveals himself to us as well in the breaking of bread at Communion.

The Upper Room

The Upper Room was a prison, not a haven for Jesus' fear-filled disciples in the first eight days of appearances (John 20:19-26). Each time he appeared they were locked inside the house. Each time he gave them his peace. It is the perfect antidote to fear. After returning from Galilee, they stayed in the Upper Room, not in fear but in trusting obedience. We too need to obey God out of trust, not fear. His peace is found in trusting in Jesus' finished work on the cross. It is why he showed his disciples his wounds. He was saying to them and us, "You can tell it is me by my wounds. They prove I died for your sins and made peace for you with God."

We need to see his wounds and trust in his finished work on the cross and not try to add to it. Showing his wounds was the first thing he did. When we come to him, our wounds and scars are the last thing we want him to see. Yet he is the only one who accepts us and loves us with all our wounds and scars. By doing this, we deprive ourselves of our healing and deprive him of glorifying his name by healing us. It is the beauty of God's love. He loves us just as we are, no matter how badly life has wounded us. But He loves us too much to let us stay as we are and wants to heal us by Jesus' wounds.

Galilee

Before and after his resurrection Jesus told his disciples to go to Galilee where they would see him. If they stayed in Jerusalem they were in danger from the religious leaders who had killed Jesus. They would be safer in Galilee. Being away from the capital removed the idea Jesus was the victorious King of the Jews, who would enter Jerusalem triumphantly and defeat Israel's oppressors. Over the forty days of appearances, he taught his disciples, so they could learn that his kingdom would be established by their witness and the Spirit's power. It would be established by his Church and they were its leaders. Jesus will come again as the all-conquering king.

The Sea of Galilee

The Sea of Galilee was the place where the disciples first met Jesus (Mark 1:16-20). On that occasion he provided a miraculous catch of fish (Luke 5:1-11). He did the same at the last meeting by the Sea of Galilee (John 21:1-23). On both occasions Peter had spent the previous night fishing and caught nothing. When we go out in life without Jesus in our boat, we will catch nothing. For the first miraculous catch of fish, Jesus told Peter to put out into deep water and drop his net. At this final miracle before his ascension, Jesus told him to drop the net on the right side of the boat. This teaches us two things: Jesus' power is best displayed when we are out in the deep and far from the comfort of the shore; and if we fish from the wrong side of the boat in life, we will catch nothing.

Fishing on the Sea of Galilee was something Jesus' disciples knew better than anything else. However, if they approached it in the way that they used to live, the results were fruitless (John 21:1-5). When they obeyed Jesus' instructions, the results were abundant. They had to put aside all that they knew and everything they had experienced to receive God's abundant provision. And it is the same for us today. We need to put Jesus' words above all that we know and have experienced in our lives in order to enjoy his fullness of life. When we are born again, we operate under a new order, the Law of the Spirit. If we return to our old ways, to how we operated before we knew Jesus as our Lord and Saviour then life will be fruitless.

When Peter came ashore he saw Jesus next to a fire of burning coals. The last time he saw a fire of burning coals was the the night he denied Jesus three times (Mark 14:66-72). It is interesting that Peter went back to the place where Jesus had first commissioned him. It was there on the shore of the Sea of Galilee that he met Jesus again and was re-commissioned. There are times when we lose our way in our spiritual lives and need to go back to the place where we first met the Lord Jesus. It is the place we need to go at times to get our spiritual lives back on track.

The mountain in Galilee

Jesus Christ, the Son of God gave the greatest set of teachings the world has ever heard on a mountain in Galilee; the Sermon on the Mount (Matthew 5:1-7:29). Also it was on a mountain where he was transfigured (Mark 9:2-13) and where his disciples saw his glory. They saw Jesus talking with Moses and Elijah. Then a cloud descended and they heard the voice of God. After the cloud lifted, they saw only Jesus. None of this would have been lost on them when they saw him on a Galilean mountain. It should not be lost on us either. The Sermon on the Mount is God's blueprint for the Christian life and the way to that life is through Jesus. He is the fulfilment of the Law and the Prophets. If we believe and remain in him and obey his teachings we will have his fullness of life.

The Mount of Olives

Jesus' last appearance was at the Mount of Olives. His disciples watched him ascend into heaven from there (Luke 24:50-51). However, the Mount of Olives was the place where Jesus had been betrayed by Judas Iscariot, arrested by the Jewish religious leaders and deserted by all of his disciples (Mark 14:32-52). At his ascension, he turned it into a place of triumph and a place of great memories for his disciples. They saw him rise to take his seat of authority at God's right hand until he returns in glory.

It seems Jesus specifically chose the locations where he appeared to his disciples after he rose from dead. It ensured his disciples' memories of those places were good and not bad. And today he will still turn the worst things that have happened in our lives into the best things that have happened in our lives, if we let him.

Have this life now

If you would like Jesus to turn the worst things that have happened in your life into the best things that will ever happen in your life. If you would like to know the Son of God who died for your sins on Calvary's cross and who rose again victorious over death. If you would like to live in the fullness of this life by trusting in Jesus' finished work and you would like resurrection life to flow through you, pray this prayer:

Lord Jesus Christ, I am sorry that I have sinned in my life and I ask that you forgive my sin through your sacrifice on the cross. I turn away from all sin. Please come and live in my heart and be Lord of my life. Fill me with your Holy Spirit. In Jesus' name I pray, amen.

If you prayed this prayer, please tell someone at your local church and contact me at thejesusdiary1@gmail.com

Appendix
Establishing a timeframe

These events took place after Jesus rose from the dead:

Resurrection events

Women visited the tomb (Mark 16:1-8 and Luke 24:1-8)
Jesus appeared to the women (Matthew 28:8-10)
The tomb guards were bribed (Matthew 28:11-15)
Peter visited the tomb (Luke 24:9-12 and John 20:1-9)
Appearance to Mary (Mark 16:9-11 and John 20:10-18)
Appearance to Peter (Luke 24:34 and 1 Corinthians 15:5)
Appearance at Emmaus (Mark 16:12-13; Luke 24:13-32)
Appearance to apostles (Mark 16:14 and John 20:19-23)
Jesus appeared to Thomas (John 20:24-29)
Jesus appeared to Peter by the lake (John 21:1-23)
Appearance on a mountain in Galilee (Matthew 28:16-20)
Appearance to Five hundred witnesses (1 Corinthians 15:6)
Jesus appeared to his brother James (1 Corinthians 15:7)
Disciples told to wait in the city for the Spirit (Acts 1:4-5)
The Ascension (Luke 24:50-53 and Acts 1:6-11)

Order and timing of resurrection events

The Scriptures say Jesus rose from the dead at dawn on the first day of the week (Mark 16:1), which was a Sunday. He rose at dawn on Sunday; the third day after he died (Luke 24: 21), which means he died on a Friday. John 18:28 says the day on which Jesus died was the Feast of Passover. Passover was held on Friday twice in this period of history – Friday, 7/4/30AD and Friday, 5/4/33AD. In my book, 'The Jesus Diary[1],' it was shown Jesus died for our sins on Friday, 7/4/30 and rose on the third day, Sunday 9/4/30. Jesus appeared to his disciples over forty days (Acts 1:3-4). Forty days from Sunday 9/4/30 is Thursday, 18/5/30. Jesus' resurrection appearances would have taken place from 9/4/30 to 18/5/30.

Women visited Jesus' tomb

Appearances began on Sunday, 9/4/30 when women went to Jesus' tomb at dawn (Mark 16:1-2; and Luke 24:1). The Jerusalem solar calendar says dawn breaks at 05:50 Hours[b] on April 9th in the current year. The time dawn breaks has not changed over the years. If it breaks at that time today, it would have broken at 05:50 Hours on Resurrection Day. When the women arrived, they found the stone moved from the entrance of the tomb (Mark 16:2-4) and inside they saw two angels (Luke 24:4). Mark 16:5 records the one who spoke. He said Jesus had risen and told them how Jesus had told them he would die and rise on the third day. He told them to tell his disciples he was going to Galilee where they would see him (Mark 16:6-7). This occurred from 05:50 Hours on Sunday, 9/4/30.

05:50 Hours onwards = Women visited Jesus' tomb

Risen Jesus appeared to the women

As the women hurried back to Jerusalem to tell his disciples, Jesus suddenly appeared to them. They fell at his feet and worshipped him. He told them not to be afraid, but to go and tell his brothers to go to Galilee where they would see him (Matthew 28:8-10). According to Matthew, these women were the first to see Jesus alive on Resurrection Day (Sunday, 9/4/30), shortly after dawn.

05:50 Hours onwards = Risen Jesus appeared to the women

The guards at the tomb

As the women went to tell the disciples, the guards at Jesus' tomb went and told the priests all that had happened. The priests and elders devised a plan. They gave the guards a large sum of money and told them to say his disciples had come in the night and stolen his body. They assured them if the report got to Pilate they would satisfy him and keep them out of trouble. They took the money and did as they were told (Matthew 27:11-15). The guards at Jesus' tomb would have informed the priests soon after 05:50 Hours.

05:50 Hours onwards = The guards at the tomb

Peter and John visited the empty tomb

The women told the Eleven Jesus was alive, but they did not believe them. Peter and John ran to the tomb. Inside they saw the strips of linen that had been wrapped around Jesus' body lying there as if he had passed through them. The cloth from around his head lay nearby, folded up by itself (Luke 24:9-12 and John 20:1-9). They would have visited the tomb on Sunday, 9/4/30 after 05:50 Hours.

05:50 Hours onwards = Peter and John visited the empty tomb

Jesus appeared to Mary Magdalene

Peter and John returned home. Mary stayed at the tomb crying. When she looked inside she saw two angels, who asked why she was crying. She said they had taken Jesus away and she did not know where they had put him. She turned and saw Jesus. Thinking he was the gardener, she asked where he had put the body. When Jesus said, "*Mary!*" she saw it was him and cried "*Teacher!*" He told her not to hold him, but to tell his brothers he was returning to his Father and their Father, to his God and their God. Mary obeyed and went and told them (John 20:10-18). The next events occurred at Emmaus after 14:50 Hours (see below). His appearance to Mary and events so far that day happened from 05:50 Hours to 14:50 Hours.

05:50-14:50 Hours = Jesus appeared to Mary Magdalene

Jesus appeared to Peter

1 Corinthians 15:5 says after rising to life Jesus appeared to Peter. On Resurrection Day, he appeared to two disciples at Emmaus who told the apostles that Jesus had appeared to Peter (Luke 23:34). If they saw Jesus that afternoon then immediately told the apostles; Jesus could not have appeared to Peter during his appearance at Emmaus. He did not see Jesus at the tomb or before he went there or he would not have run to the tomb to check (John 20:1-9). He must have appeared to Peter after Mary saw him and before he met the pair on the road to Emmaus, in the period, 05:50-14:50 Hours.

05:50-14:50 Hours = Jesus appeared to Peter

Jesus appeared at Emmaus

Mark 16:12-13 and Luke 24:13-27 say after Jesus appeared to Mary on Resurrection Day, he appeared to two disciples as they walked from Jerusalem to Emmaus. He explained to them the Scriptures concerning himself. It was nearly evening when they arrived in Emmaus (Luke 24:28-29). Evening begins at sunset. In the current year, the Jerusalem solar calendar says the suns sets on April 9th at 18:20 Hours[b]. The time the sun sets has not changed over the years, if it sets at that time today, it would have set at 18:20 Hours on the day Jesus rose to life. As they dined in the house in Emmaus, Jesus broke bread and gave it to the disciples. Then their eyes were opened; and they saw it was Jesus (Luke 24:30-32).

Emmaus was seven miles from Jerusalem. If the disciples walked at two miles an hour, it would have taken three and a half hours to get there. If they walked at three miles an hour the journey would have taken two hours and twenty minutes. As they were in deep discussion, even after Jesus joined them, it is likely they walked at a slower pace. If they arrived at Emmaus at 18:20 Hours, having walked at two miles an hour, they would have set out three and a half hours earlier at 14:50 Hours. If they walked at three miles an hour, they would have set out from Jerusalem at 16:00 Hours.

14:50-18:20 Hours = Jesus appeared at Emmaus

The disciples returned to Jerusalem

When the pair saw it was Jesus, he disappeared from their sight. They hurried to Jerusalem to tell the apostles (Luke 24:30-33). If they walked at three and a half miles an hour, it would have taken two hours to reach there. As they left Emmaus after 18:20 Hours, night would have fallen about an hour later (19:20 Hours). It would have been dark for part of the journey. If the pace dropped to two miles an hour, it would have taken up to three hours to arrive there. The journey would have happened from 18:20 Hours to 21:20 Hours.

18:20-21:20 Hours = The disciples returned to Jerusalem

Jesus appeared to ten apostles

In Jerusalem, the pair found the apostles and the others, locked in the house. As they testified that they had seen the Lord and he had appeared to Peter; Jesus came and stood among them though the doors were locked (Luke 24:33-36). After he died on Friday, 7/4/30, they had stayed locked in the house out of fear of the Jews. Jesus gave them his peace to quell their fear and showed them the wounds of his crucifixion, which they had witnessed (Luke 23:49). He ate fish then told them repentance and forgiveness of sins would be preached to all nations (Luke 24:36-48). This would have been after the pair returned from Emmaus, after 21:20 Hours. It was risen Jesus' fifth appearance on Resurrection Day, as shown below:

21:20 Hours onwards = Jesus appeared to ten apostles

Appearances in Jerusalem on Resurrection Day

1. Appearance to the women at the tomb (Matthew 28:8-10)
2. Appearance to Mary at the tomb (John 20:10-18)
3. Appearance to Peter in Jerusalem (Luke 24:34)
4. Appearance to two disciples at Emmaus (Luke 24:13-32)
5. Appearance to the disciples in the house (Luke 24:36-48)

Jesus appeared to Thomas

Thomas was absent at the first appearance to the apostles (9/4/30) but was there when Jesus appeared a week later (John 20:24-29) on Sunday, 16/4/30. At his first appearance, they were locked in the house for fear of the Jews. A week later they were still locked in there (John 20:19-26). It seems they spent the week living in fear, locked in the house. Mark 16:14 and Luke 24:33-36 say the Eleven were at that first appearance, yet Thomas was absent (John 20:24) and Judas was dead (Matthew 27:3-5). Only ten apostles were there. Either they were called the Eleven, if they were all there or not or Matthias, who replaced Judas as an apostle (Acts 1:15-26) was included. Jesus appeared to Thomas on Sunday, 16/4/30.

Sunday, 16/4/30 = Jesus appeared to Thomas

Jesus' appearances in Galilee

On Resurrection Day, Jesus told the women to tell his disciples to go to Galilee to see him (Matthew 28:8-10). It was a five-day walk from Jerusalem, so there was not enough time to make a return journey there between his two appearances in the house on 9/4/30 and 16/4/30. Jesus appeared by the lake (John 21:1-23) and on a mountain in Galilee (Matthew 28:16-20). The earliest they could have gone there was the day after Thomas saw Jesus (17/4/30).

Walking at twenty miles a day, the ninety-odd mile journey would have taken five days. If Jesus ascended from the Mount of Olives on the last day of his appearances (Thursday, 18/5/30), they would have returned to Jerusalem by Wednesday, 17/5/30 at the latest. The disciples' visit to Galilee and Jesus' appearances there would have happened from Monday, 17/4/30 to Wednesday, 17/5/30. Sabbaths and holy days would have been held in this period. As it was unlawful to walk long distances on such days (Leviticus 23:3), it would have affected when Jesus' disciples travelled.

Holy days in the period, 17/4/30-17/5/30

1. 22/04/30 = Sabbath celebration
2. 24/04/30 = New Moon Festival
3. 29/04/30 = Sabbath celebration
4. 06/05/30 = Sabbath celebration
5. 13/05/30 = Sabbath celebration

If no holy days or Sabbaths were held as the disciples travelled to and from Galilee, there are just three unbroken timeframes in which the two five-day journeys there and back could have happened:

Possible timeframes for the disciples' journeys

1. 17/04/30-21/04/30 = 5 days
2. 30/04/30-05/05/30 = 6 days
3. 07/05/30-12/05/30 = 6 days

The disciples' journey to Galilee

The disciples' journey to Galilee would have taken place from Monday, 17/4/30 to Friday, 21/4/30 or from Sunday, 30/4/30 to Friday, 5/5/30. If they had travelled from Sunday, 7/5/30 to Friday, 12/5/30 there would not have been enough time for events there to happen and for them to return to Jerusalem before the Ascension.

The walk to Jerusalem must have happened from Sunday, 30/4/30 to Friday, 5/5/30 or from Sunday, 7/5/30 to Friday, 12/5/30. It could not have occurred from Monday, 17/4/30 to Friday, 21/4/30 as that did not leave enough time for them to go to Galilee. If they walked there from Sunday, 30/4/30 to Friday, 5/5/30, it left one day (Saturday, 6/5/30) for appearances in Galilee to occur before the disciples left for Jerusalem in the final unbroken period on 7/5/30. They could not have walked to Galilee from 30/4/30 to 5/5/30, but must have travelled there from Monday, 17/4/30 to Friday, 21/4/30.

On Jesus' final journey to Jerusalem, Jericho was the last town he visited (Mark 10:46-11:1; and Luke 19:1-28). If his disciples took that route, it would have been their first stop on the way to Galilee. They would have spent Monday, 17/4/30 walking there from Jerusalem and stayed there overnight. In his ministry, Jesus went through Samaria on his way to and from Galilee (John 4:1-43 and Luke 9:51-56). It would take two days to walk from Jericho to the Galilee border.

If his disciples took this route; they would have spent Tuesday, 18/4/30 walking through Samaria. They would have stopped in a town before sunset and spent the night there. On Wednesday, 19/4/30, they would have walked to the border with Galilee and stayed in that area overnight. On Thursday, 20/4/30, they would have crossed the border, passed through south Galilee and stayed in Nazareth for the night. On Friday, 21/4/30, they would have walked to Capernaum and arrived there before the Sabbath began at sunset.

17/4/30-21/4/30 = The disciples' journey to Galilee

Order of appearances in Galilee

In Galilee, John 21:1-23 records Jesus' appearance by the lake and Matthew 28:16-20 records his appearance on a Galilean mountain. John 21:14 says the lake appearance was his third to them. The first two were in Jerusalem (John 20:19-29). The lake appearance took place before his mountain one. As 1 Corinthians 15:5-7 records five appearances, it needs to be seen when they happened:

Appearances in 1 Corinthians 15:5-7

1. Appearance to Peter
2. Appearance to the Twelve
3. Appearance to more than five hundred brothers
4. Appearance to James
5. Appearance to all the apostles

Order of appearances in 1 Corinthians 15:5-7

Paul says Jesus appeared to Peter first then to the Twelve. On Resurrection Day, the two disciples who saw Jesus at Emmaus told the Apostles he had appeared to Peter then he appeared to all who were there in the house (Luke 24:33-36). If 1 Corinthians 15:5 refers to this appearance to Peter on Resurrection Day, it was after he appeared to Mary and before he appeared to the two disciples.

1 Corinthians 15:5 says after Jesus appeared to Peter; he was seen by the Twelve. At his first appearance in the house, only ten apostles were there as Thomas was absent (John 20:24) and Judas was dead (Matthew 27:1-10). When he appeared there one week later, Thomas was there (John 20:26-29), so eleven apostles saw him that night. The number of apostles was restored to twelve after the Ascension when Matthias replaced Judas (Acts 1:15-26). He witnessed both appearances in the house. If 1 Corinthians 15:5 included Matthias in 'the Twelve' then it refers to the appearance to Thomas. If the Apostles were known as the 'Twelve,' if they were all there or not then it refers to Jesus' first appearance to them.

After Jesus had appeared to the Twelve, 1 Corinthians 15:5-7 says he was seen by over five hundred brothers then he appeared to James then to all the apostles. To find when these appearances happened we need to compare them with the appearances recorded in the Gospels. The Gospels record that Jesus appeared to all the apostles on three occasions after they had travelled to Galilee:

Jesus' appearances to all the apostles

1. On a Galilean mountain to give the Great Commission
2. In Jerusalem to tell them to wait in the city for the Spirit
3. On the Mount of Olives when he ascended into heaven

If 1 Corinthians 15:7 is the mountain appearance

If Paul is referring to the apostles seeing Jesus on a mountain (Matthew 28:16-20) then he would have been seen by more than five hundred believers and James on other occasions after his lake appearance and before his mountain appearance, as shown below:

If 1 Corinthians 15:7 is the mountain appearance

1. Appearance by the Sea of Galilee
2. Appearance to more than five hundred brothers
3. Appearance to James
4. Appearance on a mountain in Galilee

If 1 Corinthians 15:7 is an appearance in Jerusalem

If Paul is referring to all the apostles seeing Jesus in Jerusalem, it would have been when he told them to stay in the city to receive the Holy Spirit (Acts 1:4-5) or at his ascension to heaven (Acts 1:6-11). It would mean events in Galilee occurred in the following order:

If 1 Corinthians 15:7 is an appearance in Jerusalem

1. Appearance by the Sea of Galilee
2. Appearance on a mountain in Galilee
3. Appearance to more than five hundred brothers
4. Appearance to James

Others present at the mountain appearance

To find when Jesus appeared to over five hundred brothers and if it and the mountain appearance are the same event, let us look at Matthew 28:17. It says some doubted at his mountain appearance. It was the fourth time most apostles had seen him, so it is unlikely they doubted. It implies others were there. On Resurrection Day, at the house, the women told the Eleven and all the others Jesus had risen (Luke 24:9). The disciples who saw Jesus at Emmaus told the Eleven and those with them (Luke 24:33). After the Ascension, the Eleven were in the house with a hundred and twenty believers (Acts 1:6-15), and also when the Holy Spirit came at Pentecost (Acts 2:1-12).

It seems they were present on Resurrection Day, Ascension Day and Pentecost. Those filled with the Spirit at Pentecost were all Galileans (Acts 2:7). If they were the 'others' in the house with the Eleven on Resurrection Day they would have gone to Galilee with them. If they were on the mountain, some of them may have doubted. As they were there at the Ascension and at Pentecost, it implies they received the Great Commission; went to Jerusalem with the Eleven and were empowered by the Holy Spirit to carry it out.

If over five hundred brothers received his Commission, they would have gone to Jerusalem with the Eleven and been with them after the Ascension and when the Spirit came at Pentecost. But the Scriptures show it was the hundred and twenty, not them. So, the appearances on a mountain and to the five hundred brothers are separate events. After descending the mountain, the disciples may have carried out Jesus' Commission and gathered over five hundred brothers when he appeared to them. It occurred in Galilee after his mountain appearance, not en-route to or in Jerusalem, as such a big group would have drawn unwanted attention. The fate Jesus suffered may have befallen them. Next, James saw Jesus. Then all the apostles saw him in Jerusalem – either when he told them to wait in the city (Acts 1:4-5) or at his ascension (Acts 1:6-11).

Timeframe of Jesus' appearances in Galilee

If the apostles left Jerusalem the day after Thomas saw Jesus (Monday, 17/4/30), they would have reached Galilee five days later, before the Sabbath began at sunset on Friday, 21/4/30. It ended at sunset on Saturday, 22/4/30. At sunset on Sunday, 23/4/30, a New Moon Festival began and it ended at sunset on Monday, 24/4/30.

The appearance by the lake lasted two days. The disciples spent the night of one day fishing and the next day Jesus appeared to them (John 21:1-23). During Jesus' ministry, events on mountains lasted two days. When he chose the apostles, he spent the night in prayer then next day chose the Twelve (Luke 6:12-16). Jesus was transfigured on a mountain one day, but it was the next day when he descended it (Luke 9:28-37). If he appeared on one of these mountains, his appearance would have spanned two days.

As fishing and walking up and down mountains was unlawful (it was seen as work) on holy days, Jesus could not have appeared by the lake or on a mountain on Saturday, 22/4/30 or Monday, 24/4/30. Neither event could have begun on Friday, 21/4/30 and ended on Saturday, 22/4/30 nor could they have begun on that Sabbath and ended on Sunday, 23/4/30. They could not have begun on Sunday and ended on Monday 24/4/30. The earliest Jesus' resurrection appearances in Galilee could have begun was Tuesday, 25/4/30.

For the disciples to witness Jesus ascension from the Mount of Olives on Thursday, 18/5/30, they would have returned to the capital by Wednesday, 17/5/30 at the latest. The only unbroken period (when no Sabbath or holy day was held as they travelled) when they could have made their five-day journey from Galilee to arrive in Jerusalem in time to witness Jesus' ascension into heaven was from Sunday, 7/5/30 to Friday, 12/5/30. If that was when they travelled, it would mean that Jesus' resurrection appearances to his disciples in Galilee took place from Tuesday, 25/4/30 to Saturday, 6/5/30.

If Jesus' disciples stayed in Galilee from 22/4/30 to 6/5/30, Sabbaths would have been celebrated on 22/4/30; 29/4/30; and 6/5/30, whilst they were there. Also, a New Moon Festival was celebrated on Monday, 24/4/30. Those were holy days of rest. As they could not fish or climb up and down a mountain on those days it meant there were just two unbroken periods during their time in Galilee when Sabbaths and holy days were not celebrated, when these and his other resurrection appearances in Galilee could have occurred:

Timeframe of Jesus' appearances in Galilee

The 4-day period: Tuesday, 25/4/30 to Friday, 28/4/30
The 6-day period: Sunday, 30/4/30 to Friday, 5/5/30

The disciples spent the night of one day fishing. Jesus appeared to them by the Sea of Galilee the following day (John 21:1-23). They would have climbed a mountain one day and received the Great Commission (Matthew 28:16-20) then descended it the next day, if Jesus appeared to them on one of the mountains where he prayed before choosing the twelve apostles (Luke 6:12-16) or where he prayed before he walked on the Sea of Galilee (Mark 6:45-52). So his lake and mountain appearances each lasted two days. If the two appearances did not happen on consecutive days, both could not have occurred in the four-day timeframe, 25/4/30 to 28/4/30.

If Jesus' appearances to over five hundred brothers at the same time and to James happened in Galilee and both appearances took place on separate days then all four appearances would have occurred over a period of six days. If they did not take place on consecutive days, then they did not all happen in the six-day period, Sunday, 30/4/30 to Friday, 5/5/30. It would mean Jesus appeared to Peter and six other disciples by the Sea of Galilee in the four-day period, Tuesday, 25/4/30 to Friday, 28/4/30. And he would have appeared to the Eleven on a mountain in Galilee in the six-day period, Sunday, 30/4/30 to Friday, 5/5/30. An examination of these resurrection appearances in Galilee will reveal when the dates on which they occurred.

Appearance by the Sea of Galilee

Jesus' appearance by the lake could not have happened in the first three days after his disciples arrived in Galilee, due to the Sabbath celebration on Saturday, 22/4/30 and the New Moon Festival on Monday, 24/4/30. The earliest the events of his appearance by the lake could have begun was Tuesday, 25/4/30. If Peter and six others spent that night fishing and caught nothing, Jesus would have made his third appearance to them on Wednesday 26/4/30 and provided them with a miraculous catch of fish. Afterwards, he reinstated Simon Peter in his ministry (John 21:1-23).

25/4/30-26/4/30 = Appearance by the Sea of Galilee

Appearance on a Galilean mountain

Jesus' lake appearance was his third to his apostles (John 21:14). If his appearance on a Galilean mountain happened before that, John would have said his lake appearance was his fourth. If Jesus appeared to them on the mountain where he chose the Apostles (Luke 6:12-16) or on the mountain where he prayed before walking on the water (Mark 6:45-52) or on the one where he was transfigured (Luke 9:28-37), this appearance would have lasted two days. The disciples would have climbed it one day and descended it the next.

If the lake and mountain appearances did not occur on consecutive days then Jesus' second appearance in Galilee did not occur on Thursday, 27/4/30. It could not have happened on Friday, 28/4/30. If they climbed the mountain that day, they would have descended it the next, Saturday, 29/4/30. As it was a Sabbath; they would not have been able to climb down the mountain as it was seen as work, which was unlawful on a Sabbath (Leviticus 23:3). Also, the two-day appearance could not have begun on Saturday, 29/4/30 and ended on Sunday, 30/4/30 as it would have been unlawful to climb the mountain on the Sabbath. The earliest this appearance could have happened was from Sunday, 30/4/30 to Monday, 1/5/30.

30/4/30-1/5/30 = Appearance on a Galilean mountain

Appearance to more than five hundred brothers

Jesus would have appeared to more than five hundred brothers after he appeared to his disciples on a Galilean mountain. It seems that after they saw Jesus, they descended the mountain and put the Great Commission into practice. When a group of over five hundred believers gathered around them, Jesus appeared to them all at the same time (1 Corinthians 15:6). If this and his mountain appearance did not happen on consecutive days, more than five hundred brothers could not have seen Jesus on Tuesday, 2/5/30. The earliest he could have appeared to them was on Wednesday, 3/5/30.

3/5/30 = Appearance to more than five hundred brothers

Appearance to his brother James

If Jesus appeared to James (1 Corinthians 15:7) in Galilee it would have happened in the same six-day period (30/4/30-5/5/30) as his appearance on a mountain on Sunday, 30/4/30 and Monday 1/5/30; and his one to over five hundred brothers on Wednesday, 3/5/30. If his appearances did not happen on consecutive days, Jesus would have appeared to his brother James on Friday, 5/5/30.

5/5/30 = Appearance to his brother James

Journey from Galilee to Jerusalem

After his resurrection, it seems Jesus wanted his disciples in Galilee. If they stayed there for as long as possible, the last date they could have made a five-day unbroken journey (when no Sabbath or holy day was held on the way) to Jerusalem to witness his ascension was from 8/5/30 to 12/5/30. If they took his usual route through Samaria (Luke 9:51-56) and Jericho (Luke 19:1-28), they would have spent all of Monday, 8/5/30 walking from Capernaum to Nazareth. On Tuesday, 9/5/30, they would have passed through Galilee into Samaria. On Wednesday, 10/5/30, they would have walked south in Samaria and arrived in Jericho by sunset on Thursday, 11/5/30. On Friday, 12/5/30, they would have walked from Jericho to Jerusalem.

8/5/30-12/5/30 = Journey from Galilee to Jerusalem

Jesus told his disciples to stay in Jerusalem

The disciples would have arrived in Jerusalem from Galilee before the Sabbath began at sunset on Friday, 12/5/30. They would have rested in the city until the Sabbath ended twenty-four hours later at sunset on Saturday, 13/5/30. They would have spent the next four days (Sunday, 14/5/30 to Wednesday, 17/5/30) there until Jesus' ascension on his fortieth day of appearances (Thursday, 18/5/30).

In the four-day period, Sunday, 14/5/30 to Wednesday, 17/5/30, he appeared to the disciples as they ate and told them to wait in the city for a few days to receive the Holy Spirit (Acts 1:4-5), which came at Pentecost. This feast was held on the fiftieth day after the Feast of Firstfruits, which was held two days after Passover. Jesus rose to life on the Feast of Firstfruits (Sunday, 9/4/30) and he ascended to heaven on his fortieth day of appearances, Thursday 18/5/30 – ten days before Pentecost, which was celebrated on Sunday, 28/5/30. If Jesus told them to wait in the city on Sunday, 14/5/30, it was two weeks before Pentecost. If he told them on Wednesday, 17/5/30, it was eleven days before the Spirit came. He would have told them on that day to wait in the city. Any earlier and it would distort Jesus' words, *"in a few days you will be baptised with the Holy Spirit."*
17/5/30 = Jesus told his disciples to stay in Jerusalem

Jesus ascended to heaven

Acts 1:3 says that after Jesus rose from the dead, he appeared to his disciples over forty days. If he rose on Sunday, 9/4/30 then they would have seen him for the final time on Thursday, 18/5/30. That day, Jesus led them out to the Mount of Olives. Then before their eyes, he ascended into heaven to sit at God's side.
Thursday, 18/5/30 = Jesus ascended to heaven

A timeframe for Jesus' forty days of appearances is shown below:

JESUS' FORTY DAYS OF RESURRECTION APPEARANCES

S	**09/04/30**	**Jesus appeared five times in Jerusalem**
M	10/04/30	Disciples stayed in Jerusalem (Feast of Passover – Day 2)
T	11/04/30	Disciples stayed in Jerusalem (Feast of Passover – Day 3)
W	12/04/30	Disciples stayed in Jerusalem (Feast of Passover – Day 4)
T	13/04/30	Disciples stayed in Jerusalem (Feast of Passover – Day 5)
F	14/04/30	Disciples stayed in Jerusalem (Feast of Passover – Day 6)
S	15/04/30	Sabbath spent in Jerusalem (Feast of Passover – Day 7)
S	**16/04/30**	**Jesus appeared to Thomas**
M	17/04/30	Disciples travelled from Jerusalem to Jericho
T	18/04/30	Disciples travelled from Jericho to South Samaria
W	19/04/30	Disciples travelled from South Samaria to the Galilee border
T	20/04/30	Disciples travelled from the Samaria border to Nazareth
F	21/04/30	Disciples travelled from Nazareth to Capernaum
S	22/04/30	Sabbath celebration in Galilee
S	23/04/30	Jesus' disciples stayed in Galilee
M	24/04/30	New Moon celebration in Galilee
T	25/04/30	Disciples spent the night fishing
W	**26/04/30**	**Jesus appeared by the Sea of Galilee**
T	27/04/30	Disciples stayed in Galilee
F	28/04/30	Disciples stayed in Galilee
S	29/04/30	Sabbath celebration in Galilee
S	**30/04/30**	**Jesus appeared on a Galilean mountain**
M	01/05/30	Disciples descended the mountain
T	02/05/30	Disciples stayed in Galilee
W	**03/05/30**	**Jesus appeared to more than five brothers**
T	04/05/30	Disciples stayed in Galilee
F	**05/05/30**	**Jesus appeared to James**
S	06/05/30	Sabbath celebration in Galilee
S	07/05/30	Disciples stayed in Galilee
M	08/05/30	Disciples travelled from Capernaum to Nazareth
T	09/05/30	Disciples travelled from Nazareth to the border of Samaria
W	10/05/30	Disciples travelled from the Galilee border to South Samaria
T	11/05/30	Disciples travelled from South Samaria to Jericho
F	12/05/30	Disciples travelled from Jericho to Jerusalem
S	13/05/30	Sabbath celebration in Jerusalem
S	14/05/30	Disciples stayed in Jerusalem
M	15/05/30	Disciples stayed in Jerusalem
T	16/05/30	Disciples stayed in Jerusalem
W	**17/05/30**	**Jesus told his disciples to stay in Jerusalem**
T	**18/05/30**	**Jesus ascended into heaven**

Jesus' twelve appearances

Over forty days, Jesus appeared eight times in Jerusalem (on four separate days); and four times in Galilee (on four separate days):

Jesus' appearances in Jerusalem

1. Appearance to the women at the tomb in Jerusalem
2. Appearance to Mary Magdalene at the tomb in Jerusalem
3. Appearance to Peter in Jerusalem
4. Appearance to two disciples at Emmaus
5. Appearance to the apostles in the house in Jerusalem
6. Appearance to Thomas in the house in Jerusalem

Jesus' appearances in Galilee

7. Appearance to Peter and six others by the Sea of Galilee
8. Appearance to his disciples on a mountain in Galilee
9. Appearance to more than five hundred believers in Galilee
10. Appearance to his brother James in Galilee

Jesus' final appearances in Jerusalem

11. Jesus told his disciples to wait in Jerusalem for the Spirit
12. Appearance at the Ascension from the Mount of Olives

Jesus' resurrection appearances to Peter

After Jesus rose from the dead, he appeared to Peter the most times over his forty days of resurrection appearances:

1. Jesus appeared to Peter by himself on Resurrection Day
2. Jesus appeared to Peter and nine apostles in the house
3. Jesus appeared to Peter and ten apostles a week later
4. Jesus appeared to Peter and six others by the lake
5. Jesus appeared to Peter and the apostles on a mountain
6. Jesus appeared to Peter and over five hundred believers
7. Jesus told Peter and the others to stay in Jerusalem
8. Jesus appeared to Peter and the others at the Ascension

Bibliography

[1]The Jesus Diary by John Maxwell, available at Amazon.co.uk and Amazon.com

[2]Tertullian's letter to Scipio from a sermon by Dr Michael Eaton, 2012

[3]Pliny, Epistles x.96 cited in FF Bruce, Jesus and Christian Origins outside the New Testament – W.B. Eerdman publishing 1974 and Pliny, Letters translated by Rev. William Melmoth, by WML Hutchinson – Cambridge (Harvard University Press. Volume 11 x.96 cited in Habermas, The Historical Jesus 1988

[4]Suetonius, The Lives of the Caesars, Oxford World Classics

[5]Tacitus, Annals, 15.44, cited in Strobel, The Case for Christ p82 – Zondervan

[6]The Complete Works of Josephus, Antiquities, XVIII 63f Thomas Nelson 1998

[7]Babylonian Talmud, translated by I Epstein (London Soncino, 1935), volume III, Sanhedrin 43a, 81, cited in Habermas, The Historical Jesus 1988

[8]FF Bruce, Jesus and Christian Origins Outside the New Testament – WB Eerdman publishing 1974

[9]F.J.A. Hort, the New Testament in the Original Greek, vol 1, p 561, Macmillan and Co, New York

[10]Sir F, Kenyon, The Bible and Archaeology, Harper and Row, 1940

[a]Solar calendar for Jerusalem – sunrise-sunset times (excluding daylight saving hours)

Other titles by John Maxwell

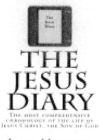

THE
JESUS
DIARY

THE MOST COMPREHENSIVE
CHRONOLOGY OF THE LIFE OF
JESUS CHRIST, THE SON OF GOD

JOHN MAXWELL

THE JESUS DIARY

THE CHRONOLOGY OF JESUS' LIFE – PART 1

'The Jesus Diary' is the most comprehensive chronology of events in the life of Jesus the Son of God ever written.

Jesus visited earth at a point in time. The Gospels give four accounts of the one story of his birth, life, death and resurrection. *'The Jesus Diary'* is Part 1 of 'The Chronology of Jesus' Life' series. It puts events of his life in the order they occurred in history. The result is the most detailed chronology of his life ever written. It helps solidify the faith of those who believe and satisfies the curiosity of those who seek to know when God walked in human form on planet Earth. It is a great aid to pastors, preachers, and Bible students, as it reveals:

- The year Jesus was born and how long he spent in Egypt
- When Jesus was baptised and his ministry began
- When John the Baptist was killed and Jesus fed the 5,000
- The hour, the day and the year that Jesus died
- The dates Jesus rose again and ascended into heaven

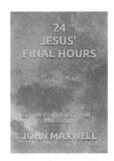

24 – JESUS' FINAL HOURS

THE CHRONOLOGY OF JESUS' LIFE – PART 2

For the first time, the final hours of Jesus' life have been set into twenty-four, hour-by-hour sections

Twenty-four hours is one turn of the Earth on its axis. Most days blend into each other, but one day changed the world forever – The day Jesus the Son of God died. All events in history prior to it led to that point and all events since then have led from that point. *24 – Jesus' Final Hours* is Part 2 of 'The Chronology of Jesus' Life' series. The revelation of what he suffered to free us all from sin has inspired me to look at his death in more detail. My hope is that in joining me on this journey of Jesus' final hours, you will discover more of the sacrificial love and selfless, giving character of Jesus as it reveals:

- When the Last Supper in the Upper Room took place
- How long Jesus prayed for in the Garden of Gethsemane
- The times of Jesus' trials and Peter's denials
- At what hour Jesus was crucified, died and was buried

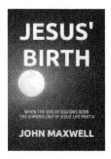

JESUS' BIRTH

THE CHRONOLOGY OF JESUS' LIFE – Part 4

A forensic examination of the information found in the Gospels regarding Jesus' birth to establish when God's Son was born.

'Jesus' Birth' is Part 4 of 'The Chronology of Jesus' Life' series. It not only establishes when Jesus was born, but it sets the existence of God on Earth in history using both Roman and Jewish historical records. Also, this book examines the 'missing years' between his birth and his baptism and what that means to us today. It reveals:

- The year Jesus was born and how long he was in Egypt
- The age difference between Jesus and John the Baptist
- When Jesus visited the temple in Jerusalem as a child
- What happened between Jesus' birth and his baptism

There is historical information in the Gospels for the time of his birth until the time he was baptised. The writer has used the information and combined it with great numeracy skills to establish the year God's Son was born in human form on Earth. Enjoy this revealing read. It will change your view of his birth, his existence and his deity.

HISTORICAL JESUS

'Historical Jesus' is the most comprehensive chronology of events in the life of Jesus, the Son of God ever written.

Jesus, God's Son visited this Earth at a point in history. The Gospels give four accounts of the one story of Jesus' ministry. *'Historical Jesus'* sets all the events of his ministry in the order they occurred and places each one on a specific date in history. The result is the most detailed timeframe of events in Jesus' ministry ever written. This chronology gives wonderful insights into Jesus' teachings, his miracles, his signs and healings and the prophecies he fulfilled. There are great insights into his relationships with those closest to him and into the hearts and minds of the main characters in his life.

Great tool for pastors, preachers and students

'Historical Jesus' helps pastors, teachers and preachers eliminate chronological inaccuracies from their sermons, which will increase the impact of their message. Also, the book is a great study aid for students of the Bible, because the book will reveal:

- The year Jesus was born and how long he spent in Egypt
- When Jesus was baptised and his Galilean ministry began
- When John the Baptist was killed and Jesus fed the 5,000
- The hour-by-hour breakdown of Jesus' final hours
- The exact times that Peter denied Jesus
- The dates Jesus died, rose again and ascended into heaven

An ideal gift for Church leaders

'Historical Jesus' is the ideal gift for pastors, leaders, preachers and lovers of the Bible as it contains a wealth of material useful for sermons and teaching. It will be a real blessing to all who receive it.

JESUS HEALS

During his time on earth Jesus preached the Good News of God's kingdom, healed the sick and cast out demons. He did so many miracles the world would not have enough room for the books that would be written (John 21:25). Only thirty-six of them are recorded in the Gospels. All Scripture is God-breathed, so the Holy Spirit, through the Gospel writers recorded them for a specific purpose. 'Jesus Heals' examines the thirty-six miracles to see what that purpose was and what it reveals about Jesus, his miracles, and his healings and how they apply to us today. This book reveals:

- The ways people came to Jesus and received their healing
- Jesus not only heals, but restores us in all ways
- Jesus has the power and authority to heal
- Jesus is willing and able to heal all who come to him
- How to receive healing from Jesus

The miracles are examined in thirty-six separate chapters. Each one reveals different aspects of God's kingdom, and the ways Jesus did his healings and miracles. It shows the faith, and the different ways people came to Jesus for healing, which inspires us to approach him in faith for our healing. Faith comes by hearing and hearing by the Word of God. As we read God's word, as we hear it and take it into our hearts, our souls and our bodies, it is Spirit and it is Life to us.

A helpful tool for pastors and preachers

For pastors and preachers, each chapter can be used as a sermon. Some miracles and healings can be put together for one talk or for a series of talks. The final part of the book summarises the miracles. After looking at the miracles, you may form your own conclusions. I pray that as you read this book, that like me, you will be healed before you finish it. If not, keep on reading until you are healed – All glory, honour and praise to God!

40 DAYS – JESUS' TEMPLATE FOR HIS CHURCH
HOW HE WANTS HIS CHURCH TO OPERATE

After Jesus' resurrection, he appeared for forty days. At each appearance, he revealed aspects of how his Church would run.

When Jesus appeared to his disciples after his resurrection, he spoke with them and ate with them. At the same time he revealed to them how he wanted his Church to operate when it began at Pentecost when his disciples were baptised with the Holy Spirit.

'*40 Days of Resurrection Appearances*' reveals the day Jesus wanted his Church to meet. It shows he highlighted to his disciples at each appearance the elements that were to be included each time his Church met – worship, prayer, prophecies; Holy Communion, miracles, testimonies and sermons that reveal Jesus in the Word. This book reveals Jesus intended his Church to be a place where all are welcome to come and seek him and to voice their doubts and have them listened to and have them turned to faith by loving and caring leaders. It shows Jesus intended his Church to be based on the words he spoke and all that is written about him in the Scriptures. He intended it to be a place of love, joy, peace, healing, restoration, giving, praise, worship and prayer. A place where miracles, signs, wonders and prophecies occurred each time his people met. The meeting was to be so full of life, joy and revelation that those who were there could not wait to share what they learned about Jesus.

The Church in many places is not operating as Jesus intended. Christian leaders and all who run churches need to return to Jesus' mandate for his Church. This book shows how Jesus intended his Church to operate. When we operate our churches in the way Jesus intended, they will be filled with people full of the joy of the Lord and the fullness of life Jesus came to bring them. Also the Church will have the full impact on the world that Jesus intended.

MY STORY, HIS GLORY

'My story, His Glory' is the testimony of the conversion of John Maxwell. In August 1994, John, who was not a Christian, went to church. He sat in a pew, disliking every minute of the experience and vowing never to go again when suddenly he felt a current of fire flow up and down his body. All his angst left him, and a wonderful peace filled him. At the end of the service the first words out of his mouth were, "I can't wait for next week." He entered the church vowing to never go again and left it eagerly looking ahead to the next service. That eagerness has never left him.

However, that was just the start of a set of extraordinary events that saw John prophesy a week later. Then he had dreams where he was taken up to heaven where he heard God both speak and laugh. After that, he had wonderful, supernatural encounters that could only have been orchestrated by God. He received wonderful words of knowledge to help others receive breakthroughs in their lives. The baptism of fire John received that day in St. Andrew's Church in Hong Kong during the movement of the Holy Spirit in the time of the Toronto Blessing is real and available to people today.

If you hunger for that fire, join John as he looks at the supernatural events that took place around his conversion. It is journey that will encourage and inspire you to receive the Baptism of the Spirit.

The ideal gift for those seeking salvation

'My Story, His Glory' is a great gift for anyone who is searching for God and eternal life or to a loved one with whom you want to share the good news about Jesus. It is the perfect reading companion for anyone doing the Alpha Course or other basic Christianity courses.

Available in hardback or paperback at Amazon.com or Amazon.co.uk

Printed in Great Britain
by Amazon

23935544R00086